A CASE FOR TEACHING LITERATURE IN THE SECONDARY SCHOOL

"This book will appeal to everyone who believes that we can learn about others and the world by reading fiction and studying great authors. Drawing on new work in cognition sciences, Alsup pushes back against Common Core State Standards typically interpreted and implemented to replace literary studies with mechanistic, less valuable, and less enjoyable approaches to learning. Present and future English language arts teachers will especially want to read this book. It is likely to become a standard in university courses in the teaching of English."

Allen Webb, Western Michigan University, USA

Taking a close look at the forces that affect English education in schools—at the ways literature, cognitive science, the privileging of the Science, Technology, Engineering, and Mathematics (STEM) disciplines, and current educational policies are connected—this timely book counters with a strong argument for the importance of continuing to teach literature in middle and secondary classrooms. The case is made through critical examination of the ongoing "culture wars" between the humanities and the sciences, recent research in cognitive literary studies demonstrating the power of narrative reading, and an analysis of educational trends that have marginalized literature teaching in the USA, including standards-based and scripted curricula. The book is distinctive in presenting both a synthesis of arguments for literary study in the middle and high school, and sample lesson plans from practicing teachers exemplifying how literature can positively influence adolescents' intellectual, emotional, and social selves.

Janet Alsup is Professor of English Education, Purdue University, USA.

A CASE FOR TEACHING LITERATURE IN THE SECONDARY SCHOOL

Why Reading Fiction Matters in an Age of Scientific Objectivity and Standardization

Janet Alsup

Routledge
Taylor & Francis Group

NEW YORK AND LONDON

First published 2015
by Routledge
711 Third Avenue, New York, NY 10017

and by Routledge
2 Park Square, Milton Park, Abingdon, Oxon, OX14 4RN

Routledge is an imprint of the Taylor & Francis Group, an informa business

Library of Congress Cataloging-in-Publication Data
Alsup, Janet.
   A case for teaching literature in the secondary school : why reading fiction
   matters in an age of scientific objectivity and standardization / by Janet Alsup.
      pages cm
   Includes bibliographical references and index.
   1. English literature—Study and teaching (Higher)—United States.   I. Title.
   PR51.U5A47 2015
   820.71'173—dc23   2014041862

ISBN: 978-1-138-82346-4 (hbk)
ISBN: 978-1-138-82347-1 (pbk)
ISBN: 978-1-315-74206-9 (ebk)

Typeset in Bembo
by Keystroke, Station Road, Codsall, Wolverhampton

For my husband, Keith, who loves to tell stories.

"And so, which is greater: the pain of the monster (the pain of the myth) or the pain of those who require their monsters? Are these mythologies, in part, the stories of our collective, or collected, pain? Or our communal hope—the kind that feeds sweat and sleeplessness? Or, to qualify, is mythology the expression of our greatest semi-imagined fears, our dumbest pain in the face of that big hope unrealized? Or is this all just a dream about raspberry mustard?"

(Matthew Gavin Frank, 2014. Preparing the Ghost.
W.W. Norton and Company, Inc.)

CONTENTS

FOREWORD

Michael Moore

In her new book, *A Case for Teaching Literature in the Secondary School: Why Reading Fiction Matters in an Age of Scientific Objectivity and Standardization*, Janet Alsup asks important questions at a time when vast changes in American education are occurring. These are new questions that challenge reform-minded assumptions. Has the mission of schools and universities shifted from providing an education to providing training and advanced training? How can educators, teachers, parents and informed stakeholders make the case for teaching vital literature in our schools and universities? What is it that happens to us when we engage with powerful literature that can change the direction of lives? What would happen to us without this literature experience? What are the forces aligning against teaching literature and what can we say to those who feel literature has less of a place in our curriculum? These are important questions and the teaching of literature is being met with open resistance. This book focuses at the heart of these questions and seeks to provide teachers with a rationale that allows them to commit to literature experiences in our schools.

Winston Churchill interviewed in the *New Statesman* in 1939 said, "Criticism may not be agreeable, but it is necessary; it fulfills the same function as pain in the human body, it calls attention to the development of an unhealthy state of things" (www.newstatesman.com/archive/2013/12/british-people-would-rather-go-down-fighting). Janet Alsup's book is in this best of traditions. She is calling attention to an "unhealthy state of things." From the start, in the Introduction she focuses on the shift made by schools and universities away from the liberal arts towards STEAM (Science, Technology, Engineering, Agriculture and Mathematics). The supposed crisis is that schools and universities are not producing enough scientists and corporations and may not have the trained skilled workers to fulfill necessary jobs. We rarely challenge such assumptions or where they come from.

In their book, *50 Myths & Lies That Threaten America's Public Schools: The Real Crises in Education,* David Berliner and Gene Glass (2014) wrote that STEM (Science, Technology, Engineering, and Mathematics) may serve the labor markets "but it is doubtful that it prepares children for a full and satisfying life" (p. 6). The authors question assumptions that we currently have too few STEM graduates, that there will be a shortage and that this shortage will cause America future problems. The STEM focus means something else has to give and Alsup notes that literature study is valued less and less by policy-makers and administrators who continue to make curricular decisions without teachers and teacher educators or other vital stakeholders. This manufactured crisis, fueled by meaningless Programme for International Student Assessment (PISA) scores and scientific organizations, has started a shift in ideas about the fundamental purpose of schooling.

As evidence, Alsup points to the Common Core State Standards (CCSS), particularly the "complex text" aspect as a scientific, as opposed to a "transactional", study of texts (see Rosenblatt, 1938, 1978). The result, as she points out, is a shift in curricula calling into question "valued knowledge and valued approaches to seeking and finding knowledge . . .". This shift is a move away from the compelling nature of narrative and its power to powerfully change identities and lives. Alan Bennett in the film, *The History Boys,* writes:

> The best moments in reading are when you come across something—a thought, a feeling, a way of looking at things—which you had thought special and particular to you. And now, here it is, set down by someone else, a person you have never met, someone even who is dead. And it is as if a hand has come out, and taken yours.

Professor Alsup starts early in her book to make the case for the future of literature and its power to "positively affect the lives of young people at the forefront." She cites the research and scholarship on narrative as particular to humanity and with evolutionary significance. In his National Public Radio (NPR) broadcast of *This American Life,* Ira Glass observed:

> There's something about narrative that we as a species are hard-wired for, in the way that we are hard-wired for language. And it enters us in a really deep way, in a back-door kind of way, in a sneaky way. And we, all of us in this room, we live in a very odd cultural moment for narrative, a moment unlike any other since there've been people in that we are inundated with narrative in a way that no people have ever been. That is . . . shows on TV, all ads are little narratives . . . songs on the radio have little stories. And one of the qualities that these narratives share, speaking for myself, I think it's really rare when there's a story . . . that feels like anything that's like my life . . . or you feel that this could be me. And when you stumble on that, a story

that can do that, it gives you a really particular feeling . . . it gives you the opportunity for empathy.

Chapter 3 is devoted to literature and empathy and the pedagogy for teaching both. Teacher educators won't find such chapters in many books. How to teach literature is very distinct from teaching empathy from literature. Alsup's sample lesson is from an actual high school English teacher and reveals the human and narrative sides of teaching literature. However, there are challenges and this book takes them on and provides teachers and teacher educators a way to conceptualize these challenges and move beyond them. Perhaps there is no greater challenge facing literature instruction today than the standards-based reform movement. These unresearched national standards at first appeared to direct English teachers in traditional classrooms to excise certain literature for expository texts. The framers of the CCSS backed off from that claim but many schools did not get this message. Additionally, the new assessments are already dictating curriculum. This book confronts and identifies these challenges.

In Part III of this book, "Reviving the High School Literary Experience," the author confronts these challenges, particularly by "Creating Readers." Readers, quite simply, pass tests. Alsup, however, moves on from these challenges and confronts literature instruction and how it affects morality. She sees this as intellectual exploration. Lionel Trilling (1950) viewed literature as promoting the moral imagination because it is teeming with "variousness, possibility, complexity, and difficulty." Janet Alsup makes the case that the public school is the best place for this to happen. This is not a "how to" book: it is a "what if" book. Few education writers are willing to engage in these muddy waters, preferring the safety of genre and conventions. However, like the students that teachers and teacher educators prepare to face, new thinking has to begin in our teacher preparation programs, our graduate schools and in our teacher development programs. We as professionals have to engage with our own literature and narrative experiences and explore ourselves as educators. This book will help the reader to do this. Merlyn's advice to the young Arthur reminds us:

"The best thing for being sad," replied Merlyn, beginning to puff and blow, "is to learn something. That is the only thing that never fails. You may grow old and trembling in your anatomies, you may lie awake at night listening to the disorder of your veins, you may miss your only love, you may see the world about you devastated by evil lunatics, or know your honor trampled in the sewers of baser minds. There is only one thing for it then—to learn. Learn why the world wags and what wags it. That is the only thing which the mind can never exhaust, never alienate, never be tortured by, never fear or distrust, and never dream of regretting."

(White, T. H., 1966, p. 183)

Janet Alsup's book, *A Case for Teaching Literature in the Secondary School: Why Reading Fiction Matters in an Age of Scientific Objectivity and Standardization,* is one of those places where you can learn something.

References

Berliner, D.C. & Glass, G.V. (2014). *50 myths & lies that threaten America's public schools: The real crises in education.* New York: Teachers College Press.

Rosenblatt, L. (1938/1995). *Literature as exploration.* New York: MLA.

Rosenblatt, L. (1978). *The reader, the text, the poem: The transactional theory of the literary work.* Carbondale, IL: Southern Illinois University Press.

Trilling, L. (1950). "Preface," *The liberal imagination.* New York: Viking Press.

White, T. H. (1966). *The once and future king.* New York: Berkeley Medallion.

PREFACE

I have been thinking about the ideas in this book for many years, even though I may not have been consciously aware of it. Or, more accurately, I didn't understand how all the issues and concerns swimming (and often colliding) in my brain were connected—literature, cognitive science, the privileging of the STEM disciplines, and obstructionist, even combative, educational policies. But these things felt related to me, felt as if taken together they might teach a bigger lesson, an important lesson that clear articulation would reveal. Writing this book has been my attempt to fit these pieces together, to articulate these connections so that English teachers and English teacher educators might argue more effectively for the value of their discipline, and, more specifically, for literary study as a means of encouraging the aesthetic and personal growth of adolescents. I hope I've succeeded in some small way.

There are three parts in this book. Part I, "What Literature Can Do," comprises four chapters which provide an overview of the positive effects literature can have on readers, as determined and explored in research and scholarship. Literature can affect readers in four ways: through identification with characters, through the fostering of empathetic response, through increased critical thought, and, finally, by encouraging increased philanthropic behaviors. Included at the end of each chapter is at least one related sample lesson from a secondary school teacher who has taught literature in ways that encourage adolescent growth in both intellectual and emotional/social domains. These lessons exemplify the type of literature teaching that I argue is important, perhaps vital, for adolescents to continue to experience. There are more examples of such lessons and activities at the end of the book, in Appendices A and B.

Part II, "Challenges to Literary Study," provides more detail and discussion about some of the barriers to continued literature teaching in our schools, namely standards-based education, or education that privileges teacher and school accountability over student learning. To exemplify these barriers, I provide a short case study of one school in my own community, a school I call College Town Middle School, and their teachers' struggles teaching literature in a school focused on standardizing daily lessons to meet the objectives of the Common Core State Standards.

Part III, "Reviving the Secondary School Literary Experience," revisits the arguments in the Introduction and takes them to the next level, attempting to answer such questions as how English teacher educators can best prepare new secondary school literature teachers, why literary study may be particularly important to adolescents and why, given all the evidence, the study of literature may be more important now than ever. The book concludes with a discussion of literacy and morality.

Janet Alsup

ACKNOWLEDGEMENTS

I would like to thank the early reviewers of this manuscript who provided useful and substantive suggestions for making the book better. I also want to express special thanks to Routledge publisher, Naomi Silverman, who has always listened to my ideas and responded to them wisely. Thanks, Naomi, for your continued support and encouragement. Finally, I thank the students in my spring 2014 young adult literature class at Purdue University, who helped me explore many of the issues included in this book.

1

INTRODUCTION

The Need to Make the Case for Teaching Literature

As an English education professor in a university known for science, engineering, and agriculture, some days can be pretty demoralizing. It seems that daily I read in university communiqués some new praise of the so-called STEM or STEAM ("A" being agriculture, not the arts) disciplines, side-by-side with some subtle, or even overt, denigrating of my own. And not only does the verbal praise keep drifting the way of STEM and STEAM, so do the monetary prizes. In fact, a series of new initiatives at my university is designed to put more money, energy, and faculty hours toward the science and technology disciplines, while there is little mention of the liberal arts. When questions are asked about the place of the liberal arts at the university, the response is that we are important supporters of the STEM students and faculty, as we can help them communicate more effectively about science and technology. There's little acknowledgement that knowledge made, found, and explored in the humanities can add anything, on its own, to human knowledge or culture. There's little recognition that the humanities have any independent, contemporary relevance to human life.

Twenty years ago when I became a high school teacher I never imagined that I'd be exploring the question, why teach literature? I never thought the day would come when I would be compelled to write a book defending the inclusion of literature in the high school and middle school curriculum and, by association, the importance of adolescents engaging in literary experience. But today there is increasing evidence that literature is being valued less and less by policy-makers and administrators making decisions about what is taught in public middle and high schools, despite a recent National Endowment for the Arts (NEA) report that literary reading is "on the rise" among adult Americans, particularly young adults between the ages of 18 and 24, reversing a two-decade downward spiral in reading (*Reading on the Rise*, 2008). While the reasons for this upswing are unclear—I might argue that the surge in popularity of young adult novels might have something to do with it—it is evidence that even in the so-called digital age young people are choosing to read.

Describing and explaining the epistemological, philosophical, and economic battles between the humanities and the natural sciences has been attempted before (a quick review of research will bring up such names as Dewey, Kuhn, Nussbaum, and Bérubé). It's an intimidating group of scholars to be following, to say the least. So why do I wish to add my thoughts to the mix?

What this book offers is a conversation about *secondary school* language arts and literature instruction and the literary experience. I argue, through the lenses of philosophy, cognitive science, literary studies, and educational policy studies, for the reading and teaching of literature in the middle and high school. Finally, I provide specific classroom applications for the teaching of literature that are consistent with these theories. In sum, the purpose of this book is to add to the current conversation about the place of the humanities in general, and literature teaching more particularly, in contemporary secondary education and to argue that the study of literature has an important place in our schools, and, by extension, in our lives.

Since the time of the ancient Greeks, the questions "What is worthy knowledge?" and, by association, "What is the definition of truth?" have been debated. In fact, questions such as "What is science?", "What is nature?", "What is beauty? truth? art? and even, "the meaning of life?" have all been explored since the beginning of real human thought—since the first human primates were able to think abstractly and imaginatively as well as concretely and literally. As soon as the human brain was able to move beyond "How do I live through this day?" to "How do I make my existence more complete?", we have been grappling with the questions, "Which complete is more complete?" and "Which way of knowing is the most worthy or worthwhile?". As Varki and Brower (2013) write:

> The one thing that does seem to separate us from other animals is that we are capable of going beyond self-awareness of our own personhood to having a full theory of mind (i.e., full *awareness of the self-awareness and personhood of others*).
>
> *(p. 39)*

However, ironically, it took the industrial revolution, and the supposed modernization of society, to reduce the level of such questioning to a simplistic either-or dichotomy. It was in the 19th century that Western scholars began to create divisions among bodies of knowledge and the consequent disjuncture between so-called humanistic and scientific knowledge (Wallerstein and Lee, 2004, p. 3). It was also during this time that literature became a school subject (Langer, 2014, p. 161). For the record, the ancient Greeks did not see a clear distinction, much less a battle, between the humanities (i.e., literature, art, aesthetics) and the natural sciences (i.e., biology, chemistry, knowledge that can be discovered empirically); they, in fact, saw them as acting together, as interdependent types of knowledge, each affecting and enriching the other. It seems that simplistic dualism is a relatively recent phenomenon, as the separation of academic and scholarly study into categories, what we call disciplines, is still the norm today and arguably often leads to competition among those disciplines—for both prestige and resources. In a famous lecture in 1959, British scientist and novelist C.P. Snow described for the first time the epistemological conflict between the sciences and the humanities. He was the first to call these two types of knowledge "cultures" and the first to argue that their division was harming society. Interestingly, in his time, he saw the humanities as unfairly valued and rewarded at the expense of the natural and practical sciences. How times have changed.

So how did the sciences and related understandings of objectivism, empiricism, and truth vault to the top of the valued knowledge chart in the 21st century? How did it become the case that politicians, policy-makers, and corporate execs (and school administrators) use numbers and statistics, what they might call objective knowledge, to make arguments that affect people and social institutions, such as health care, food quality, and, our main topic here, education? As David Hollinger argues in a review in *The Chronicle of Higher Education* (2013), today's culture wars between the sciences and humanities are as much about the intellectual and political, *content* of scholars' work as they are about abstract definitions of truth or knowledge. In the 1980s and '90s it became a relatively common critique of humanities professors that they were too politically correct and too entrenched in left-wing sentiment to do rigorous, evidence-based research (see Bloom, 1987 and, for a rebuttal to Bloom, Bérubé, 2006). Such arguments increasingly positioned humanities scholars as subjective and engaged in research to advance personal/political agendas rather than to advance human thought or teach students valuable information.

However, scientific data may not always be the best way to make decisions that affect people. Daniel Sarewitz of the Center for Science and Technology Policy Research at Arizona State University studies how policy decisions based on scientific research can affect human problems—sometimes adversely. In "Liberalism's Modest Proposals, Or the Tyranny of Scientific Rationality," Sarewitz (2012) criticizes "scientific rationality unchecked by experience, empathy, and moral grounding" and argues against the "false belief that right action can be extracted from a set of scientific facts" (unpaged). Instead, he posits that we must seek a balance between science and humanism—pay equal attention to both scientific fact and informed human experience.

Regardless of such arguments, hard facts and data have become the preferred way to understand education in the US. We've probably all seen the National Center for Education Statistics (NCES) charts comparing the knowledge of students in the US with those in other countries. The Program for International

Student Assessment (PISA) measures 15-year-olds' performance in reading, math, and science every three years and compares these measures across nations. After doing some research, I found an NCES document stating that in 2009, "the average reading literacy score in the United States was lower than the average score in 6 of the 33 other OECD (Organization for Economic Cooperation and Development) countries, higher than the average score in 13 of the other OECD countries, and not measurably different from the average score in 14 of the OECD countries" (http://nces.ed.gov/fastfacts/display.asp?id=1). While this seems to place us in a pretty solid position at first glance, many political pundits use variations of this information (changing comparison countries, for example) to argue that US public education is failing. For example, in a recent *Bloomberg Businessweek* article, alarmingly called "The Real Reason America's Schools Stink," author Charles Kenny writes, "the US ranks behind sixteen other economies including Poland, Estonia and South Korea in terms of student literacy—the ability to read, integrate and evaluate texts" (2012, unpaged). Since the article does not have a works cited or references page, I can't really tell where these numbers came from or how they were calculated. But they certainly sound bad, and they seem like evidence for drastic change. Regardless, the numbers are presented as objective truth.

As I was writing this chapter, the 2012 PISA (Programme for International Student Assessment) scores were announced, again showing that the US "performed below average in mathematics" and "performance in reading and science are both closer to the OECD average" (www.oecd.org/pisa/keyfindings/PISA-2012-results-US.pdf). Since the US has a much more diverse (and in many cases, larger) population than many of the countries on the OECD list, such as Japan, Portugal or Luxembourg, one might think this assessment not too alarming. However, many news outlets reported on the crisis purportedly revealed by these scores. For example, Education Secretary Arne Duncan in a *Washington Post* article called the scores a "brutal truth" that "must serve as a wake-up call" for the country (Lyndsey, 2013). Diane Ravitch did a thorough oppositional reading of the scores in her blog post of December 3, 2012. In part she writes:

> If they mean anything at all, the PISA scores show the failure of the past dozen years of public policy in the United States. The billions invested in testing, test prep, and accountability have not raised test scores or our nation's relative standing on the league tables.
>
> *(http://dianeravitch.net/2013/12/03/my-view-of-the-pisa-scores/)*

She goes on to question why we should care about the test scores anyway, as they only measure rote learning and not imagination, creativity, and the ability to innovate.

Setting aside the literal difficulties of figuring out where such numbers come from or how they are calculated, the numbers are themselves an oversimplification that cannot reflect the true reality of complex social, cultural and behavior issues at work in an American school. As Gaukroger (2012) writes:

> It is not so much that quantification—in this case, the reduction of things to raw numbers, to statistical regularities, so that everything can be put on the same level and compared—becomes tantamount to objectivity. It is not even so much that such objectivity now becomes a tool for micro-management. Rather it becomes a form of control that allows complete abdication of responsibility.
>
> *(p. 74)*

This evolution in what is considered valued knowledge and valid approaches to seeking and finding knowledge is affecting not only state and national social and educational policy, but also what happens at the local, public school level. In English language arts classes around the nation, standards and curricula are becoming more rigid and discussions of teacher and school accountability are rampant, resulting in changes in the very nature of how English teachers define their jobs. One specific result is that literary study, namely the study of fictional texts, drama and poetry, is decreasing (or at best remaining constant), and the focus on non-fictional, informational texts is increasing. Increasingly, reading and writing informational texts that are "complex" is replacing narrative writing and reading because, the argument goes, such texts better prepare students for life after high school. The recently created Common Core State Standards (CCSS), now adopted by 44 states, emphasize the teaching of so-called informational or non-fiction texts, especially in secondary school English, and make a strong argument that all texts that are taught should be "complex" according to their definition. The standards define text complexity as "the inherent difficulty of reading and comprehending a text combined with consideration of reader and task variables" (CCSS, 2012a). The standards go on to provide a three-part measurement for text complexity that takes into consideration qualitative, quantitative, and reader/task considerations (CCSS, 2012c, *Supplemental Information for Appendix A*, p. 4). I wrote in a recent commentary that appeared in the *Journal of Adolescent and Adult Literacy* about this new way of defining classroom-worthy texts:

> Such ways of measuring the complexity of literature and the literary experience for readers is certainly new for English teachers, and some teachers and administrators are viewing this method as a devaluing of traditional fiction, particularly longer novels which take significant class time to read. Some secondary educators are deciding that reading long fictional works may not be the best use of time if student experience with

multiple, interdisciplinary, "complex texts" is the goal, particularly for middle and high school readers who are urged in the CCSS to read more nonfiction than fiction

(CCSS, 2012d, Revised Publishers' Criteria, Grades 3–12, p. 5
Alsup, 2013, pp. 181–182)

No matter what one thinks of the new definition of what makes a text worthy, it is hard to argue that such a formula for measuring text complexity is far removed from many of the ways English teachers, professors, and even prolific readers of literary texts currently think about the value of a text or how they would explain a reader's experience with literature. It seems many miles from Louise Rosenblatt's (1938/1995, 1978) discussion of the transaction between the reader's experience and the words on the page. Like so many things in US education today, this process for analyzing text complexity reduces the quality of the literary experience to a triangular formula that can be determined through objective analysis, rather than a "to-and-fro spiraling" (Rosenblatt, 1938/1995, p. xvi) between the reader and the words on the page. Rosenblatt's assertion that no critical interpretation of a text can happen without a prior, aesthetic, lived-through personal experience with it, seems to have been reduced to one part of the text complexity triad, called "reader/text considerations." Lexile scores based on counting sentence and word lengths are given equal importance in the CCSS. The experience of reading has become virtually dehumanized.

So why do we have to make a case for teaching literature? Why does it matter? I argue at a time when the humanities seem to be losing the culture war, when the standardization and objectification of the educational and literary experience of our youth is rampant. English teachers and English teacher educators must keep discussions about the power of literature to positively affect the lives of young people at the forefront. We should argue that all worthwhile knowledge isn't objective, that all things worth learning cannot be relegated to, or assessed by, a formula. If we wish our young students to become citizens of the world who can make ethical decisions about the many scientific discoveries, ecological challenges, and human tragedies coming across the newspapers daily, we must nurture and preserve their opportunities to experience narrative worlds, as characterized by Richard Gerrig in 1993. And perhaps more specifically related to the daily lives of adolescents, the literary experience, intimately connected to the building of empathy, may be an essential part of slowing the spread of such social problems as bullying, school violence, and rampant uncivil discourse. Reading literature is perhaps now more important than ever in an age of dehumanizing and fleeting images, decontextualized policy making, and mass shootings that speak to a lack of empathy in our culture at large.

In the rest of this chapter, I provide a brief overview of some of the major foundational concepts explored in the book. First, I discuss what I mean by the digital age, or the age in which we are living now, in the year 2013. Second,

I provide a brief historical overview of the cultural conflict between the sciences and the humanities that began in the 19th century and continues today. Third, I explore a related philosophical concept essential to understanding how contemporary knowledge and truth are understood by Americans and American policy-makers: the twin notions of objectivity and subjectivity. Finally, in the remainder of the book I lay out some questions about how literature and literature teaching may be understood through these historical and cultural lenses, and continue to explore the concept of literature teaching and learning.

Living in the Digital Age: What It Is and What It Means

There is no doubt that the nature of knowledge has changed over the last several hundred years, as well as how we find it. In just a few short decades, we have moved from the set of encyclopedias and card catalogs on 3 x 5 index cards to Google and Wikipedia to find our answers. It has, of course, taken many years for the means of production in our nation to move from the industrial revolution to an information-driven economy, but we can see signs of the change everywhere: from the bankruptcy of the Michigan automobile companies to the increasing disappearance of the middle class, and the rapid automation of jobs that used to require human labor. The types of job that are valued in contemporary US society, as well as how we are educated to perform them, have changed greatly and continue to change. Interestingly, even though the nature of the jobs that high school and college graduates will be asked to perform has become more and more complex, popular sentiment about schools, driven by media and political discourses of practicality and consumerism, often expresses discontent that secondary schools and colleges aren't preparing graduates to get well paying jobs immediately after graduation. At my own institution, as in many others, there is frequent talk of providing "more education for the dollar" and making sure we attract students who are apparently shopping among an array of educational options in order to make sure they are positioned to cash in on the highest possible earnings during their lifetime. Funny, though, that I rarely have a student in a class tell me that is his or her goal.

Arguably, the onset and current dominance of this digital age are connected to the predominance of scientific knowledge as the preferred knowledge form. As we become more dependent on technology and computers for our day-to-day lives, we easily become convinced that these technologies are providing us with indisputable facts and the objective information that we need to do many things, ranging from making our own medical diagnoses to writing an English literature paper. We eagerly await new scientific/technological advancements, such as the new iPhone, the new tablet or the latest gaming system. Although our lives can revolve around the technology that we love and value, most of us don't really understand its inner workings. However, we trust it, sometimes implicitly, sometimes so much that we believe it provides us with indisputable, virtual experiences and knowledge. This may be especially true for our youth, who must often be taught that all knowledge found on the Internet is not equally true. Digital technology, despite its enormous potential benefits, increases the likelihood of knowledge oversimplification and the all-too-ready digestion of inaccurate and incomplete knowledge—and it might be said that it was created out of the very kind of scientific knowledge it espouses. Perhaps it's true that "Google [is] making us stupid" (Carr, 2008).

I am not a technophobe. I have a smart phone, use a computer daily, and tweet. You may be thinking at this point that I am about to set up a divide between knowledge of the digital age and that of the humanities. The disjuncture, and sometimes even battle, between human and technological knowledge has been well documented in everything from popular culture to scholarly essays; it has been realized in the daily life of educators representing both fields. However, the humanities and the digital age are not necessarily and essentially divided or at odds. Interesting connections continue to be made frequently in teaching, research and even artistic productions such as movies, music, and art. We see principles related to aesthetics and beauty showing up in corporate decision making, with Apple Computers being a key example of a company designing products with the visual, kinesthetic, and even auditory pleasure of the consumer in mind (see Don Norman, 2005). However, the increase in digital technologies and the reliance on them in all aspects of life has changed the way we think about truth and the types of knowledge we value. If we rely on digital technologies for every other aspect of our lives, from personal communications to professional habits and obligations, it seems natural that Americans would see science and technology as our savior and our current and future reality. And where exactly do the humanities, and specifically the study of literature, fit into this technological, digitized world? Perhaps nowhere. Perhaps everywhere. Time will tell.

The Culture Wars: Science Versus the Humanities in Perspective

As mentioned earlier in this chapter, there is a history of the humanities and the sciences being at odds. I certainly see this controversy in my world today, as an English professor in a research university dominated by the STEM disciplines; daily, I receive e-mails and research funding invitations that are about advancing research and knowledge in the sciences, technology, engineering and mathematics. I find myself wondering if the liberal arts even exist any more, and if they do what and whom do they serve? The numbers of students in our English department continue to decrease at undergraduate level, and we find ourselves increasingly concerned about how we can justify our existence to our administration and, by extension, to parents and taxpayers. Our knowledge and ways of knowing have become suspect; they are not rigorous or clear or straightforward, or, most importantly, objective. Many people think we are just about political correctness and identity politics.

In the 19th century, when the disciplines as we knew them were created, there were scientific breakthroughs that vaulted the natural or hard sciences to dominance, including such life-changing discoveries as Ohm's law of electricity, the Doppler effect, Joule's first law of thermodynamics, Darwin's theory of evolution by natural selection, and Mendel's laws of inheritance. Even the basis for quantum theory was uncovered, and the path was laid out for Albert Einstein's theory of relativity to emerge in the early 20th century. The hard sciences were expanding and exploding fast, in all realms: biology, physics, chemistry, and mathematics. As respect and esteem for the natural and hard sciences expanded, the respect and esteem for the humanities correspondingly decreased. As Wallerstein and Lee (2004) write:

> It seems clear to us that in this nineteenth-century struggle the scientific culture was able to impose itself socially as the dominant culture in the world of knowledge of the modern world-system. The degree of its supremacy seems to have been a steady upward curve until it reached a high point in the period 1945–1970.
>
> *(p. 4)*

Wallerstein and Lee also argue that from the 1960s to the end of the 20th century the humanities made some progress in this cultural battle. They write that "seven major intellectual movements from the 1960s to the end of the 20th century affected the supremacy of the sciences: complexity studies, social studies of science, diversity movements (feminism, race, ethnicity), popular culture/cultural studies, and ecology/environmentalism" (p. 4). However, as much as I would like to believe their claim that the humanities are regaining some power in the knowledge market, my daily experiences tell me differently. It seems that in the mid-21st century the humanities have begun a downward slide again, to the point that foreign language and philosophy programs in universities are being cancelled, majors are decreasing, and emphasis is placed on increasing and retaining those skilled in STEM disciplines, at the expense of the humanists.

In the last few years there have been many much-hyped articles and editorials about how the humanities are failing or declining (or not), including Verlyn Klinkerborg's *New York Times* piece (2013) "The Decline and Fall of the English Major," in which Klinkerborg defends the humanities and states that despite recent struggles, he would like to see more English majors because of what they can offer to business and culture. On the contrary, Michael Bérubé in the July 2013 *Chronicle of Higher Education* disputes that humanities enrollments are dropping at all and calculates the numbers a little differently than the critics, who tend to be annoyed by English departments' recent emphases on race, class, and gender studies. Bérubé argues that if we look at the enrollment numbers in the humanities over time, the decline actually waned around 1980. Since then, according to his reading, numbers are up a bit, even though the narrative of the dying English major continued heartily. So there is disagreement even among those in the humanities about the extent to which we are in crisis, who is creating or publicizing this crisis, and for what reasons.

However, to demonstrate the point that American culture has begun to value scientific, objective numbers and arguments even in the field of education at the expense of other more humanistic ones, I will point to some examples. First, new ways of viewing teaching performance at the K–12 level value countable dimensions of teaching, behaviors that can be placed into charts and graphs and viewed in comparison to other teachers. Such charting and comparison has been done to the secondary school students for a very long time; we have all seen the newspaper reports comparing the test scores of our local schools so we can determine which schools are better—and which are worse. This way of valuing performance has now become a reality in teacher evaluation—and even entire school evaluation. My home state of Indiana is currently debating a revised "A though F" rating system for our public schools (the first system was overturned after evidence arose that scores were not being determined "objectively"). The new teacher evaluation system in Indiana is linked to merit pay for these teachers, and is called "RISE" (seems like an acronym but, interestingly, I could find nowhere what it actually stands for). This system takes into consideration "multiple measures", including teacher practice and student performance, as determined from standardized testing, to provide a "picture of an educator's performance" (Indiana Department of Education, 2013). RISE then "identifies strengths and areas of improvement, which can help teachers grow year after year." In RISE teachers are scored on a four-point scale, from "ineffective" to "highly effective" as based on a series of numerical rubrics—the "teacher effectiveness rubric" has three domains, plus a "core professionalism" rubric that equals a total of 15 pages; all are rated on the four-point scale, with the domains "weighted" differently (instruction is the most valued domain, followed by leadership and then planning). The entire evaluation results in a "summative rating form" which tallies the numbers for a "final summative rating." Then you know how good a teacher you are. At last. Thank goodness.

The second example of scientific thinking running the educational show at the expense of humanistic knowledge comes from my own experience at the university where I teach—a major public university in the Midwest geared toward math, science, technology, and engineering—with a healthy dose of management and pharmacy thrown in for good measure. I recently received a document in my e-mail inbox titled, "fostering and assessing student growth." OK. Sounds good. How do we do this? In this document, student growth is quantified and understood through the scientific lens of empiricism: we can test and we will know—about everything, from personal proclivities to content knowledge. The ultimate goal is developing the "T-Shaped" student who is defined as:

> the individual who possesses deep disciplinary-competence, as well as breadth in knowledge and personal skills. The T-Shaped student is one

who has experienced significant growth during undergraduate study and is well prepared for success in making a living and making a life.

("Fostering and Assessing Student Growth," Purdue University, 2013, p. 2)

Creating, and assessing (which seems paramount to effectively creating) such a student involves getting "baseline performance" measures, "longitudinal performance" measures, and "benchmarking" (p. 3), or comparing our students to those at other universities. All three components of a T-Shaped student (personal development, intellectual growth, and disciplinary competence) can be assessed through quantitative measures, according to this document: Gallop polls, the collegiate learning assessment (CLA), and various Educational Testing Service (ETS) disciplinary tests, which would, of course, be purchased. This model of the T-Shaped student assumes that all aspects of a well-rounded human being can be measured with and through numbers; that all knowledge of value can be quantified and reported to others in the form of numbers or statistics displayed in charts and graphs, and that it is of utmost value to compare decontextualized students to each other to find out what they really know and who they really are.

Third, and last, as mentioned earlier in this chapter, within the Common Core State Standards (CCSS) document, assessing the quality of literary texts has become a matrix, a rubric, to assess the level of "text complexity" that a certain text exhibits. The higher the ratings of "text complexity" the better the text, and the more excited teachers should be to teach it. The measurement for text complexity is based on "three factors": "qualitative evaluation of a text, quantitative evaluation of a text, and matching reader to text and task" (CCSS, 2012b). The qualitative factors include "levels of meaning, structure, language conventionality and clarity, and knowledge demands," the quantitative, "readability measures and other scores," and matching reader to text means "reader variables" such as who students are and what they like to read about. The whole thing can be understood by looking at this triangular graph containing these three measures. I never knew reading a novel could be so similar to solving an algebraic equation.

When we look at the epistemological conflict between the sciences and the humanities, we can also understand it as a conflict between ways of thinking and knowing about the world at large—a conflict between positivism, or the belief that there is an external validity or singular truth that can be found, and the belief that knowledge is created or constructed, often with the assistance of personal, intuitive or reflective thought. While many contemporary scientists would dispute the fact that they do not value intuition or personal experience or reflection (and they are right in that such a conception of their work is an oversimplification), I would argue that this dualism is widely accepted in educational and social/cultural institutions and it has affected the very nature and structure of our schools and universities.

Objectivity and Subjectivity: How Science Became Truth

The very basis of the science/humanities debate seems to be the nature of truth itself and, by association, objectivity, which has become synonymous with truth. In contemporary US culture, the word "objective" is often used to mean true, or real, or not shaded by emotion or personal experience which would muddy the waters and obscure the truth. When someone says in general conversation that a piece of information is objective, it means to most that it is probably true, based on facts and not personal opinions which are always, in contrast, "subjective," meaning untrue, emotional, personal, and naturally suspect.

However, Stephen Gaukroger disputes that objectivity means without judgment or personal interpretation; he argues that discussions of objectivity can only arise when informed judgments and personal interpretations are involved. He writes about the conflation of objectivity and truth, "There are two problems with this conception. First, the idea that we are being guided towards *the* truth is wholly misleading. What we are being guided towards are the best answers to the questions that we pose" (2012, p. 66). Regardless, objectivity has become a synonym for accuracy and truth, and scientific knowledge is often viewed as objective—and, hence, the truth.

This conflation of truth and objectivity, and now objectivity and scientific thought, began in the late 16th and early 17th centuries as notions of truth as the end point of intellectual thought shifted to a sense that objectivity was the ultimate goal of knowledge as well as the path to find real knowledge. In other words, if we pursue knowledge with no bias or preconceived ideas, then truth will result, an objective, *real* truth (p. 59). However, truth and objectivity are different things; one is absolute and the other comes in degrees (p. 66); one may be shaped by informed judgments and personal experiences, the other must resist these personal influences.

Regardless of philosophical problems conflating truth with objectivity, it seems to have become the norm in our society, as the goal has come to be objective in order to be truthful. One can see this notion in the responses of readers to non-fictional texts that turn out to be fictionalized, such as Frey's *A Million Little Pieces* (2003) or Wilkomirski's Holocaust "memoir" *Fragments: Memories of a Wartime Childhood* (1996). Frey wrote a book marketed as a memoir about his drug addiction, but later had to publicly apologize on the Oprah Winfrey show when it was discovered that all his claims were not literally true. Wilkomirski was likewise caught in the act of writing a memoir including events that didn't really happen when a Swiss journalist discovered that he wasn't really a child in two different concentration camps during World War II. However, even if some literal experiences were not factually described, does this mean the books contain no truth at all? Do either texts contain any emotional or personal truths? Both men argued that their texts were still true in many ways. The general public didn't think so as both authors were stripped of awards, publishing contracts, and their dignity. Frey's publisher Random House offered refunds to readers who felt betrayed. But what is a memoir any way? Who controls how someone else re-constructs and expresses his or her memories? If a literal event is not depicted as it may have actually occurred, does that make the memoirist's retellings without merit?

Interestingly, on a later episode of her show, Oprah apologized to Frey for ambushing him and implied that maybe she had oversimplified the notion of truth in memoir after all. Maybe she realized that truth can indeed sometimes be subjective. That truth with a capital "T" may comprise feelings, emotions, and personal interpretations—even flawed memories, in addition to just the facts. Or maybe she just felt guilty for leading Frey to public humiliation. It's hard to say. Regardless, both controversies demonstrate that the American public values the notion of truth as objective, untarnished with personal, muddy subjectivities, even when people narrate personal stories. If subjectivity or inaccuracy in representation is noticed, the author is shamed and labeled as a deceiver.

Truth in the humanities is not objective, nor does it claim to be. In fact, scholars in the humanities would argue that personal, or subjective, knowledge is central to the search for real truth, or meaning. However, in an age when objectivity connotes fairness, honesty, and even truth, and subjectivity indicates bias, prejudice and partisanship, it is becoming harder to argue that study of the humanities, and its hallmark subject, literature, is important or worthy.

The Literary Experience

So how can literature solve all these problems? Isn't that very notion exaggerating its potential a bit, even if one likes to read? In the next chapter I begin exploring this issue in more depth, but, in sum, there has been much research in the last decade about how literature can affect and foster empathy, identification with others, and, most recently, actual altruistic human behavior.

Much research and scholarship concerning the power of literature to change identities has been based on the body of research and scholarship about narrative: storytelling as a powerful way to develop self. This research from the disciplines of psychology, sociology, anthropology, education, and literary studies is not primarily concerned with fictional narratives or literary texts, but with personal narratives, memoirs, autobiography, life stories, or just the internal stories we tell ourselves about who we are. Many scholars have theorized that storytelling is what makes us human; the ability to tell stories, make up stories, and understand our own experience and relate it to others via stories is specific to the human animal and has evolutionary significance. While humans haven't always written novels or short stories, it is arguable that since the evolution of human consciousness people have fashioned, told, and re-told stories of their own and others' lives. These stories have had a number of purposes: to teach lessons, to remember events, to entertain, to celebrate, and even warn of danger. When the first novels and narrative poems were written we moved into the age of text, and our stories became documents that could be saved for generations. It was then that the experience of storytelling became even more central to human life and human experience. There are some who argue that it is because of stories that we have survived as a species, and storytelling might very well keep us alive into the future. Stories are how we remember and share essential cultural and personal knowledge.

Theory of mind is a concept relating to the idea that we are all "mind readers" of a sort; the functional human, who is able to interact with others in an effective way, is skilled in the ability to intuit or read what others may be thinking or feeling and make an appropriate response. This isn't to say that we are actually reading the exact thoughts of others, as in a science fiction movie; however, we can often sense the feelings and motivations of others based on body language, facial expressions, statements, and our experience in other situations, both real and vicarious. As written in the introduction to Leverage et al. (2011):

> Theory of Mind (ToM) is what enables us to "put ourselves in another's shoes." It is mind reading, empathy, creative imagination of another's perspective; in short, it is simultaneously a highly sophisticated ability, and a very basic necessity for human communication.
>
> *(p. 1)*

Scholar Lisa Zunshine has linked this ability with the literary experience, and many theorists have followed her: reading literature both enhances ToM skill and ToM is necessary for effective literary reading. She argues, "reading engages and improves mind reading abilities" (Leverage et al., 2011, p. 2).

Social imagination is a related concept, often synonymous with ToM: social imagination is the ability to put yourself in the place of others, imagine what their situations must be like, temporarily take on their perspectives, and empathize with them, even though they may be unlike you in many ways. Theorists of social imagination likewise argue that the literary experience both exposes and enhances social imaginative abilities (see Lysaker and Miller, 2013).

Perhaps an umbrella concept encompassing both ToM and social imagination is realized in cognitive literary studies, which emerged as a field of study in the 1980s (Jaén and Simon, 2012, p. 13). In their book, *Cognitive Literary Studies: Current Themes and New Directions*, Jaén and Simon define the field as "an interdisciplinary initiative that integrates humanistic and scientific approaches and methodologies into a powerful tool to explore the complex dynamics between cognition and literature" (p. 13). In addition to the broad areas of ToM and social imagination, more specific areas of study falling under the cognitive literary studies domain include neuroscience and how the brain reacts to reading or experiencing narratives, how reading or narrative experience can influence the identities, empathies, and even literal behavior of readers, how narrative experience might have evolutionary significance for individuals and the human race at large, and how the teaching of literature might deepen literary and related cognitive-emotional experiences.

In the following chapters, I will delve into these areas of study in more detail and begin connecting their findings and the knowledge they have revealed to the larger issues of knowledge construction and reception, the work of the humanities, and recent developments in contemporary US education. Perhaps the field of cognitive literary study and related scholarly endeavors are simply a defensive reaction on the part of humanists to justify the veracity of their knowledge by adopting the very scientific methods with which they are in competition; or, perhaps these studies are revealing what many of us have known intuitively about literary study for years: reading and experiencing narratives changes readers—how they feel, think, and interact with others.

The High School Literature Teacher

The daily job of the high school literature teacher may seem far removed from conversations about the future of the humanities, the nature of knowledge and truth, and research about how the reading of literature can affect cognition and emotion. However, there are many connections, and I think understanding the bigger picture, the history and philosophy behind decisions made today about classroom curriculum, assessment, and school organization, can help those of us who teach English and work in teacher education more clearly define our challenges and seek solutions that will make a difference.

What are some of the challenges facing the high school literature teacher today? Challenges exist on a number of levels, beginning with literal, local classroom problems such as student motivation, classroom management and overworked teachers. Then there are larger school and district issues that often morph into policy concerns, including interpreting scores on standardized tests, conducting teacher evaluations linked to merit pay, negotiating often negative perceptions of schools in communities, and dealing with any number of legal and policy mandates ranging from transportation, to school safety, lunch menus, and the curriculum. While teachers may not make the ultimate decisions on any of these issues, the decisions that are made impact the daily life of the teacher and, by association, the daily experience of his or her students. At the district or school level, literature teachers may also have to deal with censorship cases involving challenged books, many of them young adult novels, and text selection controversies. It's more important than ever for these teachers and their students to make a cogent argument for the teaching of literature that is grounded in historical thought and reality, policy analysis, scholarly research, and anecdotal teacher knowledge.

References

Alsup, J. (2013). Teaching literature in an age of text complexity. *Journal of Adolescent and Adult Literacy, 57*(3), 181–184.

Bérubé, M. (2006). *What's liberal about the liberal arts? Classroom politics and "bias" in higher education.* New York: W.W. Norton and Company.

Bérubé, M. (2013). The humanities, declining? Not according to the numbers. *The Chronicle of Higher Education,* July 1. Retrieved from http://chronicle.com/article/The-Humanities-Declining-Not/140093/

Bloom, A. (1987). *The closing of the American mind: How higher education has failed democracy and impoverished the souls of today's students.* New York: Simon and Schuster.

Carr, N. (2008). Is Google making us stupid? What the Internet is doing to our brains. *The Atlantic.* Retrieved from www.theatlantic.com/magazine/archive/2008/07/is-google-making-us-stupid/306868/

CCSS (National Governors Association Center for Best Practices & Council of Chief State School Officers) (2012a). *English language arts Appendix A.* Washington, DC: Authors. Retrieved from www.corestandards.org/resources.

CCSS (National Governors Association Center for Best Practices & Council of Chief State School Officers) (2012b). *English language arts standards: Standard 10: Range, quality, & complexity. Measuring text complexity: three factors.* Washington, DC: Authors. Retrieved from www.corestandards.org/ELA-Literacy/standard-10-range-quality-complexity/measuring-text-complexity-three-factors

CCSS (National Governors Association Center for Best Practices & Council of Chief State School Officers) (2012c). *Supplemental information for Appendix A of the Common Core State Standards for English language arts and literacy: New research on text complexity.* Washington, DC: Authors. Retrieved from www.corestandards.org/resources

CCSS (National Governors Association Center for Best Practices & Council of Chief State School Officers) (2012d). *Revised Publishers' Criteria, Grades 3–12.* Washington, DC: Authors. Retrieved from www.corestandards.org/resources

Frey, J. (2003). *A million little pieces.* New York: Anchor.

Gaukroger, S. (2012). *Objectivity: A very short introduction.* Oxford, UK: Oxford University Press.

Gerrig, R. (1993). *Experiencing narrative worlds: On the psychological activities of reading.* New Haven, CT: Yale University Press.

Hollinger, D.A. (2013). The wedge driving academe's two families apart: Can STEM and the human sciences get along? *The Chronicle of Higher Education,* October 14. Retrieved from http://chronicle.com/article/Why-Cant-the-Sciencesthe/142239/

Indiana Department of Education (2013). RISE: Evaluation and Development System. Retrieved from www.riseindiana.org/how-does-rise-work/overview

Jaén, I. & Simon, J. J. (Eds.) (2012). *Cognitive literary studies: Current themes and new directions.* Austin, TX: University of Texas Press.

Kenny, C. (2012). The real reason America's schools stink. *Bloomberg Businessweek,* August 19. Retrieved from www.businessweek.com/articles/2012-08-19/the-real-reason-americas-schools-stink

Klinkerborg, V. (2013). The decline and fall of the English major. *The New York Times,* Sunday Review, June 22. Retrieved from www.nytimes.com/2013/06/23/opinion/sunday/the-decline-and-fall-of-the-english-major.html?_r=0

Langer, J. A. (2014). The role of literature and literary reasoning in English language arts and English classrooms. In K.S. Goodman, R.C. Calfee, & Y. M. Goodman (Eds), *Whose knowledge counts in government literacy policies? Why expertise matters,* pp. 161–167. New York: Routledge.

Leverage, P., Mancing, H., Schweickert, R. & William, J. M. (2011). *Theory of mind and literature.* West Lafayette, IN: Purdue University Press.

Lyndsey, L. (2013). US students lag around average on international science, math and reading test. *The Washington Post*, December 2. Retrieved from www.washingtonpost.com/local/education/us-students-lag-around-average-on-international-science-math-and-reading-test/2013/12/02/2e510f26-5b92-11e3-a49b-90a0e156254b_story.html

Lysaker, J. & Miller, A. (2013). Engaging social imagination: The developmental work of wordless book reading. *Journal of Early Childhood Literacy*, 13(2), 147–174.

National Center for Education Statistics (2013). Fast facts. Retrieved from http://nces.ed.gov/fastfacts/display.asp?id=1

NEA (National Endowment for the Arts) (2008). *Reading on the Rise: A New Chapter in American Literacy*. Washington, DC.: National Endowment for the Arts.

Norman, D. (2005). *Emotional design: Why we love (or hate) everyday things*. New York: Basic Books.

Programme for International Student Assessment (PISA) (2013). Results from PISA 2012—United States key findings. Retrieved from www.oecd.org/pisa/keyfindings/PISA-2012-results-US.pdf

Purdue University Student Growth Task Force (2013). *Fostering and assessing student growth*. West Lafayette, IN: Purdue University.

Ravitch, D. (2012). Diane Ravitch's blog: A site to discuss better education for all, December 3. Retrieved from http://dianeravitch.net/2013/12/03/my-view-of-the-pisa-scores/

Rosenblatt, L. (1938/1995). *Literature as exploration*. New York: MLA.

Rosenblatt, L. (1978). *The reader, the text, the poem: The transactional theory of the literary work*. Carbondale, IL: Southern Illinois University Press.

Sarewitz, D. (2012). Liberalism's modest proposals, or, the tyranny of scientific rationality. *The Breakthrough*. Retrieved from http://thebreakthrough.org/index.php/journal/past-issues/issue-2/liberalisms-modest-proposals/

Varki, A. & Brower, D. (2013). *Denial: Self-Deception, False Beliefs, and the Origins of the Human Mind*. New York: Twelve.

Wallerstein, I. & Lee, R.E. (2004). *Overcoming the two cultures: Science versus the humanities in the modern world-system*. Boulder, CO: Paradigm Publishers.

Wilkomirski, B. (1996). *Fragments: Memories of a wartime childhood*. New York: Schocken.

PART I

What Literature Can Do

What can literature do? This might seem an odd question, as literature is not a sentient being and cannot *act* on or in response to anything. Regardless, fiction has undeniable effects on readers, effects that are realized and reported both in anecdotal experience and published research. Literature is not just read, or consumed; it can be a catalyst for personal change.

Beginning here, each of the three part openers includes a story or two, narratives about narrative, contributed by a friend, fellow teacher or student. I hope these short stories reinforce the theme of each section—here, what literature might do—and model how fiction can be as powerful as fact.

Bellies and Books

I can still feel and smell William's brand-new baby skin as we curled up in the pillow and I read him his very first book, perhaps just a few hours in this big, beautiful world. Speaking in rhythm and fluctuating tones, we shared those gifts that come as stories. This was a gift I could not and would not wait to give him. The gift of animals, trucks, and faraway places, turning the pages, the passage of time, discovering patterns of language, and the way pictures danced on pages. The opportunity to spend quality time unwrapping tales and learning of life that exists beyond the rails of his crib. Now, in the quiet morning sun that shines through the window just above my shoulder, William jumps down from the rocking chair and sifts through his basket of books. At just eighteen months old *he* is choosing what we read. With one hand out to balance, he uses the other to sort through the tumble of books in the basket. I watch. I wait. I observe his selection process. He picks out a book that is thick and sturdy. One we have read many times over. He picks, *I Love You, Stinky Face*. A book that is not quick, a book that talks of emotions and dialogue between a mother and her son. I smile. Not because I am pleased with his selection, but in his passion to hear a story. His desire to sit nestled in my lap and turn the pages himself as he has learned to listen for pauses. I smile knowing when he will make certain gestures and noises as he has become familiar with the style of predictable books. I smile because each time we do this, he unwraps the gift of story.

By Kelly Shaw

Reference

McCourt, L. (2004). *I Love You, Stinky Face*. Scholastic Inc.

My favorite book(s)

When I think back to my history with books, I struggle with identifying the *one* that spoke to me. I was a big reader as a kid but when I was about 11, a librarian asked me what I wanted for Christmas. I said books and became embarrassed, realizing that she had expected a different answer. Didn't she see the stacks I had been taking home? Why did she look so confused by my answer? Or was I somehow weird? The weird girl who liked to read.

Realizing there was some stigma around being a girl who read too much, to this day, I have a hard time telling someone what my "favorite" book is. I think I'd say Shirley Jackson's *We Have Always Lived in the Castle*, a book I discussed in my undergraduate thesis. It's about two sisters living in the house where the rest of their family was poisoned within a community that ostracizes them. It's a weird book. I get it. I was a teenager who could lose herself in books. I think maybe the reason I have such a hard time with this question is because it says something about me. My favorite book. What a personal question. With my answer, I'm going to tell you so much.

There's this picture of me that I've always liked. I'm 13, sitting in a bikini in my Nan's backyard. My glasses are at the edge of my nose, my face is scrunched up, and I'm staring down at this giant book. I wish I could tell what book it is. It would tell me so much about who I was. That's what I love about books, not one in particular, but the way that what I'm reading always speaks to who I am at one particular moment.

By Brittany Biesiada

Reference

Jackson, S. (1962). *We have always lived in the castle*. New York: Viking Press.

2

LITERATURE AND IDENTIFICATION

How Self Becomes Character

We all—adult and children, writers and readers—have an obligation to daydream. We have an obligation to imagine. It is easy to pretend that nobody can change anything, that we are in a world in which society is huge and the individual is less than nothing: an atom in a wall, a grain of rice in a rice field. But the truth is, individuals change their world over and over, individuals make the future, and they do it by imagining that things can be different.

(Gaimon, N., 2013, p. 9)

When I read a work of fiction, it's often the extent to which I identify with a character that determines how much I like it. If I don't see some aspect of myself, or anything or anyone that I care about, I am not likely to continue reading. Alternatively, if I see too much of myself, or anything or anyone that I care about, I also might not continue reading, but for a different reason. If the book makes me feel too much, so much that reading is difficult, I may choose not to engage with it. I may decide to postpone the reading until later, until my present reality has changed enough to allow an easier reading experience, or I may decide that the book will never be a text that I can easily digest. Alternatively, finding a book with characters, settings, or events with which I identify can bring great pleasure, joy, and even a series of personal epiphanies. In short, reading fiction is very personal for me.

Others seem to feel the same way. I belong to a neighborhood book group in the town where I live. We choose books together and meet once a month to discuss the books, eat various hors d'oeuvres, and drink wine. At a meeting a couple of months ago, one of our most reliable members didn't read the book, which was unusual. (This time the book was Khaled Hosseini's *And The Mountains Echoed*, a novel about love and loss within generations of a family.) When we asked why she opted not to read the book this time around, she replied that her son had recently had a psychic break and was in the hospital for much of the last month; she was simply so sad she couldn't read the book—or any fiction for that matter.

I found this to be a poignant, and fascinating, revelation. I, also, have found myself too sad (or angry or frustrated) to read fiction for pleasure, no matter what the subject matter or topic. The novel didn't have to be about exactly what I was going through—the very act of allowing myself to enter the emotional world of a narrative was just too vulnerable a proposition; I didn't feel secure enough to put my emotions on the line by reading a novel. To me, and apparently to my friend in the writing group, fiction is that powerful. So powerful that sometimes you can't even read it.

What is Identification?

In my years of teaching high school, I often noted how adolescents would have consistently similar answers to the question, why did you like (or dislike) the book? Their answers would often be something like, "I could (or couldn't) relate to it." They evaluated the effectiveness of a novel based on how much they identified with it.

However, it often seemed that their brand of identification meant a pretty close one-to-one correspondence between their personal identities and the identities of the character(s) in the books they were reading: if the characters (or even the setting) were too different from themselves, too alien to their own lives and experiences, they would often reject the text as not interesting, not understandable, not fun to read, and simply not for them. In a recent *New Yorker* opinion piece, Rebecca Mead calls such literary response "the scourge of relatability," and sees the contemporary tendency to judge texts based on "the extent that the work functions as one's mirror" as a "failure that has been dispiritingly sanctioned by the rise of the 'relatable'" (2014). Perhaps Mead is correct and the increase in valuing the relatability of texts is connected to a modern, Western tendency (or need?) to see the self reflected and reaffirmed everywhere. However, she does make the point that knee-jerk relatability is different from thoughtful identification.

Norman Holland (1975) wrote about how relationships with texts may change over a lifetime as a reader gains life experience. His theory of psychological "identity themes," or areas of interest that stem from real-life events, posits that our personal interests and concerns color our readings of literature—in his words: "we each transform the resources the work offers us so as to express our different identity themes" (p. vii). Perhaps as we grow older and amass more life experiences, our ability to "transform" the resources of a narrative to parallel our own needs and interests is heightened; consequently, we may not so quickly dismiss a book because its surface features are not immediately recognizable.

Regardless of how processes of identification might change over a lifetime or with more experience, identification seems to be at the very heart of reading narrative fiction. It must occur if the reader is to engage with the text, be motivated to read it, and get anything real, or significant, out of it. Louse Rosenblatt (1938/1983) and Ben Nelms (1988) (among others) have written that a personal response or aesthetic experience must occur prior to an interpretive, analytical, or critical one. Perhaps what both were really getting at was this idea of identification—a reader needs to identify with a character, setting, or series of events in order to empathize with said characters, engage in interpretation or criticism, and perhaps, ultimately, be moved to think or act differently as a result of the vicarious experience. The reader must first identify in order to fully experience Gerrig's so-called "narrative world" (1993). Gerrig argued, among other things, that identification with characters enhances the emotional responses of readers who can respond to fictional texts as sincerely as they might respond to nonfictional ones, even sometimes changing their behavior or beliefs in response to a story (pp. 193, 198). The process of identification simulates real life emotions that might result in real life actions, as depicted in the visual image below.

There are many ways to define identification. Woodward (2003) defines it as "the conscious alignment of oneself with the experiences, ideas, and expressions of others" (p. 5). Holland (1968/1975) goes a step further, describing character identification when reading as a type of "projection and introjection" during which readers take on character qualities, but also inject their own beliefs into those of the characters (p. 278).

The concept, if not the word, may have been first used to describe a psychological experience by Sigmund Freud, who in 1897 theorized the process of identification with a parent as a type of emotional, sometimes unconscious, assimilation of the parent's characteristics or attributes (see "On Narcissism,"

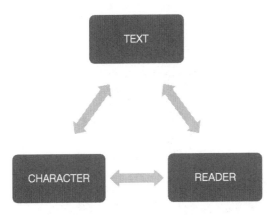

FIGURE 2.1 The process of literary identification. Identification during literary reading involves interaction between a text, its characters, and the reader.

1925). Some of the earliest discussions of identification and texts occurred more than two thousand years ago with Plato's denouncement of poetry for its ability to arouse unhealthy emotions through simulated, or imitative experience, and Aristotle's rejoinder that such emotional responses to narrative can actually result in healthy, cleansing catharsis. Somewhat later, C.S. Lewis problematized the notion of identification, especially among the young, in his famous "On Three Ways of Writing For Children" (1952/2002) in which he argues that fantasy literature can have a greater effect on both children and adults than so-called "school stories" which attempt to depict the lives of children. Fantasies are somehow able to communicate greater, deeper personal truths through the adventures of mythical creatures and fairies than the exploits of characters drawn by authors attempting to mimic real life. Fantasy, or fairy tale, contains archetypes that allow young readers to exit real life for a while, with its associated fears and disappointments, and enter a fairy realm where they can imagine, create, and confront fears vicariously.

As I mentioned earlier, many times when I was teaching high school, young readers would base their like or dislike of a book on two criteria: whether they could identify with the main character (or not) and whether the book seemed real, which seems to me now to be just another way of talking about identification. If the book is realistic, that means the reader can see his or her life within it; if he or she can relate to or identify with the characters or events, then the book is realistic. For a long while I was frustrated by these responses, because I thought they were a simplistic view of reading—so readers can't like a book if the characters are unreal, or live in a fantasy world, or take the form of an animal, alien being, or hobbit? It seemed to be an excuse for avoiding any piece of literature that wasn't striving for social realism.

What I think I misunderstood about my students' responses was that they were not arguing that a book had to have a realistic setting or a character that looked and acted exactly like them—but instead that they had to find some point of connection, something that made the book or the characters real for them, something they could remember or understand from their own lives, within the story. Once this connection was found, the real reading experience could commence. As a reader becomes more skilled, nimble and experienced, it may be true that such identifications can become more abstract, subtler, less obvious or literal—perhaps even easier to achieve. But even with practiced adult readers, if the connection cannot be found, if identification cannot be made on some level, the book is often lost and the reading abandoned.

In the late 1940s and early '50s, scholars and educators continued to write about identification, fiction, and how reading might change readers. Bley (1945) wrote in *The English Journal* that as a reader becomes more skilled and experienced and reads increasingly "successful" and well-written texts, the reader's process of identification with characters and settings becomes richer, more complex, and more thoughtful (pp. 28–29). He argued that identification is not just a base or non-intellectual act of believing oneself to be similar to a character one likes;

instead it is at the very heart of why every reader reads and why every writer writes; it is both intellectual and emotional, as well as being critical and personal:

> Identification is not a device of "escapist" literature, used by irresponsible writers as bait for inadequate readers; it is a process inherent in the purpose of every author of fiction. It is absent from a fiction-reading experience only when author or reader has failed in his purpose.
>
> *(Edgar S. Bley, 1945, p. 27)*

Russell and Shrodes (1950) wrote about a concept closely related to identification, bibliotherapy, the notion that reading books, particularly the right books, can help a reader know himself or herself better, work through problems and challenges, and grow emotionally:

> If there is a genuine therapeutic effect from reading, it may be explained theoretically in terms of *identification, catharsis,* and *insight,* terms originating in psychoanalytic literature but now more widely accepted by psychologists. In such terms, bibliotherapy becomes a process of identifying with another character or group so that feelings are released and the individual develops a greater awareness of his [*sic*] own motivations and rationalizations for his [*sic*] behavior.
>
> *(p. 336)*

Identification is a doing; it is an act. It happens around us every day, even when we don't read. When we engage in a casual conversation we are engaging in identification—we are listening to what the other says to us, trying to understand his or her main point or perspective, trying to figure out how we will respond or communicate. Why do we feel uncomfortable when a friend or family member we love is shamed or embarrassed? Because we identify with them—they are a part of us, we are a part of them. Why is it sometimes difficult to watch a TV show or movie, clearly labeled as fiction, when a character does something we know is going to end badly or if the character will not survive? It's probably because we are identifying with that character. Some people seem more prone to engage in such identification; others seem able to shut off this process and engage with narrative texts, as well as everyday reality, with more emotional distance. Others seem to be identifying with everyone and everything around them, whether human, animal, or even vegetable. Thompson (2010) calls such people "extreme empaths," individuals who empathize so strongly they routinely experience the same feelings of others, even if they would prefer not to (p.1).

Aristotle saw identification as an essential part of the art of rhetoric. As Woodward writes, Aristotle "convincingly places the roots of communication in the impulses of common ground and assimilation" (p. 5). Aristotle's concept of ethos can easily be understood as an impulse to identify with the speaker, as well as a call to the speaker him or herself to develop a character or characterization that can be believed (or identified with) by the listener—that is, if the speaker wishes to persuade. Of course, misused identification as a rhetorical tool can become dangerous, a form of emotional control over others. If you can get a listener or reader to believe your message, if you can convince them to identify with you or your followers, you may be able to change their actions. A good example of identification for the purpose of control is advertising; who can't identify with someone who wants shinier hair or fresher breath or clearer skin? If you identify with the spokesperson, or the testimonial, you must act in a similar way: buy the product they are extolling. If you identify with the experiences and messages of a political candidate, you may vote for him or her. Remembering the 2012 presidential race between Mitt Romney and Barack Obama, identification was certainly an issue at play. Not many could identify with the wealthy corporate executive Mitt Romney, who seemed out of touch with the lives of most middle-class Americans; however, we could identify with how Obama was narrativized in the media and by his campaign staffers: the man who fought for communities in Chicago, who grew up in a diverse multi-racial, single-parent family. What happened? We voted for Obama.

But I don't want to focus on the negative possibilities of identification; instead I want to focus on the positive. By identifying with others, both real and fictional, we are better able to communicate, deal with conflicts and problems, and find creative, mutually beneficial compromises. It can be argued that identifying with others has evolutionary significance for humanity; by identifying with other people and their experiences, we can understand them better and learn from them; by identifying with characters and events in stories we can learn about things that might help and harm us vicariously, before these things actually happen. We can stave off poor decisions. And, of course, having other people identify with us allows us to form more complete, productive, and full identities; people are often lost and lonely in a world where they think their experiences are unique; the typical adolescent mantra of "you just don't understand me!" is a human plea for someone to identify and communicate this identification. And a time when identification seems to most readily happen, when it is commonly labeled and noticed, and can be examined and interrogated, is when fiction is read. In the next section of this chapter, I discuss what we can learn from scholarly and academic research about reading fiction and the emotional–intellectual process of identification.

Researching Identification

So how do we know what identification is, what it can do, and how it occurs? In my research, I found many scholarly articles and books about identification and reading reaching back to the 1930s, with scholars such as Louise Rosenblatt (1978, 1983), David Russell (1949), C.S. Lewis (1952) and Edgar Bley (1945). Clearly interest in and thinking about how narrative can inspire identification with listeners or readers is not new. It continues to be of primary interest as teachers try to motivate young readers to read and interrogate their identification processes. In addition to educators, psychologists, anthropologists, literary scholars, and cognitive scientists are likewise interested in the intellectual and emotional processes of identification. Today's research is interdisciplinary, both empirical and theoretical, and supplemented by recent neurological research leading to insights about what happens in the brain when we read fictional narratives.

In the earliest work, scholars and theorists wrote about the process of identification in a purely theoretical way—how, after much careful thought and observation, they assumed the process worked. These scholars, including Rosenblatt, Russell, Lewis, and Bley (and later Robert Probst and Alan Purves) spoke from their own experience as readers and, often, as teachers of literature. Looking at the second edition of the *Handbook of Research on Teaching the English Language Arts* (Flood et al., 2003) it is clear that research throughout the '80s and '90s focused on general areas such as literary theory and criticism, qualitative or ethnographic studies of readers and reading sites, qualitative or descriptive studies of social contexts surrounding reading (such as families, institutions such as schools and governments), studies of early language learning and reading, and studies of how readers from different cultural and social backgrounds relate with texts. Recently, with the increasing popularity of cognitive literary studies, or what some call neuroaesthetics or neurohumanities, researchers have added an empirical dimension, exploring through quantitative, qualitative, and mixed method studies what happens in the brain or "mind" when readers confront narrative, fictional texts. These studies, which tend to focus more on reader personality change and the emotions of readers, try to explain what many of the early theorists believed intuitively and through experience: reading literature changes readers.

The field of cognitive literary studies emerged in the 1980s and has integrated new knowledge in neurology with literary scholarship and educational research on reading processes. One such neurological discovery with implications for the teaching of literature is the identification of so-called "mirror neurons" that work in conjunction with other neurons in the brain and that fire not only when certain actions are performed, but also when a person witnesses or observes actions performed by others. These neurons have been linked to the limbic system, which controls feelings and emotions (Alsup, 2013, p. 183; see also Gallese & Goldman, 1998; Iacoboni, 2005; Iacoboni, 2008; and Rizzolatti & Craighero, 2004 on the subject of mirror neurons.) It's possible that simulated, narrative experience could also trigger mirror neurons, particularly when the reader vividly imagines story events.

As mentioned in the Introduction, Jaén and Simon (2012) describe cognitive literary studies as "an interdisciplinary initiative integrating humanistic and scientific approaches and methodologies into a powerful tool to explore the complex dynamics between cognition and literature" (p. 13). This field exemplifies one way in which the sciences and humanities might come together to better understand a basic human process and experience, even if all scholars on both sides of the research divide do not agree on the usefulness of the work. Some "hard" scientists see humanists as misreading and oversimplifying neurology; some humanists dispute that they need to take on the epistemologies of the natural sciences in order to discover important knowledge. Regardless, the work in cognitive literary studies has shed a great deal of light on the benefits of reading literature as explored in this book, including identification, empathy, and prosocial behavior.

Related to the work above is the overriding idea that reading literature influences the mind in positive ways and can make us emotionally, empathically, and personally more aware, tolerant and understanding. In other words, reading literature can increase our emotional intelligence. As mentioned in the Introduction, the idea of "theory of mind" is central here. Lisa Zunshine (2006) has written that increasing mind reading skills is why people read and why people have read for centuries. In essence, reading and experiencing narrative worlds helps human beings get along in the real world, with real people, more effectively.

Thinking about identification specifically, there are some interesting studies of note. Perhaps most recently, Richter, Appel, and Calio (2014) conducted a study in which they asked young women to read a story about the life of a young mother. After reading, they asked the female readers to rank themselves on a "femininity" scale. They found that the participants who read the story about the mother, a traditional gender role, rated themselves more highly on the femininity self report, particularly if they were engaged with the story and they weren't currently parents. The researchers conclude that exposure to the narrative changed the women's self-perceptions. Expanding examination of the effects of reading stories to relationships with others, David Comer Kidd and Emanuele Castano (2013) conducted a study in which they discovered that reading literary fiction, as opposed to nonfiction or popular fiction, leads to better performance on tests of ToM. In other words, reading fiction enhanced the "mind reading" abilities of participants who were asked to read various kinds of texts and then complete measures of their emotional IQ, such as describing the emotions they see in photographs of pairs of eyes or inferring fictional characters' emotions. Kidd and Castano write:

> We submit that fiction affects ToM processes because it forces us to engage in mind-reading and character construction. Not any kind of fiction achieves that, though. Our proposal is that it is literary fiction that forces the reader to engage in ToM processes.
>
> *(p. 1)*

Why is literary fiction different from other types, such as what Kidd and Castano call "popular" fiction? They explain: "Miall and Kuiken (pp. 15–17) emphasize that through the systematic use of phonological, grammatical, and semantic stylistic devices, literary fiction defamiliarizes its readers" (p.1). Defamiliarization requires readers to slow down, read more carefully, and think about the author's message. Hence, time and space is provided for identification to occur. I would argue that much of the fiction we ask young people to read in secondary schools, whether it be canonical, contemporary, or young adult, could be viewed as "literary" according to Kidd and Castano's definition, as it contains many foregrounded figures of speech and devices, such as metaphor, simile, metonymy, alliteration, and symbolism.

Raymond Mar and Keith Oatley's idea of reading literary narratives as a type of simulation of social experience also speaks to the concept of identification. They argue in their 2008 article, "engaging in the simulative experiences of fiction literature can facilitate the understanding of others who are different from ourselves and can augment our capacity for empathy and social inference" (p. 173). They write that like a computer simulation of an activity or event, reading a narrative is a simulation of real life experience, one that happens in the mind, even though real thoughts and emotions may result. To fully engage in a narrative, a reader projects him or herself into the story as if the story were real; the reader vicariously experiences events and feelings, while simultaneously realizing they are abstractions that only exist as copies of reality. Regardless of this realization, learning and personal growth can result. A large part of such engagement and projection is dependent upon identification with characters. Mar and Oately write:

> In experiments with short stories by Alice Munro and Ambrose Bierce, Kerr (2005) found that identification with a main character increased literary involvement as measured by the number of emotions readers experienced while reading the stories . . . Thus, understanding characters in a story is a means through which we can come to better understand ourselves and others.
>
> *(p. 182)*

Feeling empathy towards characters in literary texts might result in changed attitudes toward others, and perhaps even increased altruistic or prosocial behavior, although research about effects on behavior is still rather slim. (I'll discuss the available research linking reading to prosocial behavior in Chapter 5.) The first step toward empathy and related reader growth is, first, reading the literature and second, identifying with the characters and events in a fictional world. In this way, a reader is both lost in a text (Nell, 1988) and, ultimately, found in one.

The Pedagogy of Identification

Critical pedagogy

The last sections of each of the chapters in Part I of this book will focus on how the concepts and theories explored in the particular chapter can be related to literature teaching, or the actual classroom translation or application of the idea. While there could be many ways to realize a particular concept or psychological/ intellectual process (such as identification) in classroom practice, in each case I choose one that I find particularly relevant and consistent with the essence of the concept. In this first case, I have chosen critical pedagogy as an effective pedagogical approach to encourage young readers' complex identification with characters in fiction. In the sections below, I briefly define the approach, focusing first on its theory and then on possible practical enactment. Second, I connect the pedagogy to the concept under discussion, as it is explicated earlier in the chapter, including relating it to the previously provided visual process model representing my understanding of how the cognitive/affective process might actually occur with students.

What is critical pedagogy?

Critical pedagogy is an educational philosophy, which, by employing fundamental components of critical theory, seeks to encourage students to become conscious of the pervasive hegemonic power within their culture and society, power that often unfairly privileges some people and groups over others. Through this critical awakening, students ideally are moved to take real-world action (i.e., praxis) to create positive change. Well-known theorists of critical pedagogy include Freire (1968/2000), Giroux (1981), hooks (1994), Apple (1996), Shor (1980) and McLaren (1995), among others. Some have critiqued critical pedagogy on the grounds that either it is basically impossible as long as traditional school structures remain that place the teacher at the center of the classroom with pass/ fail power, or it is dangerous as students could be traumatized by unforeseen, radical shifts in worldview or by the realization of the fragility of their seemingly ordered world. Some even claim the aim of critical pedagogy is to produce young anarchists. A related concept is bell hooks' "engaged pedagogy," which, while perhaps not as based on uncovering hegemony and exposing injustice, calls for the teacher and students to be co-learners of sorts, learning from each other in a mutual educational mission (1994, 2003).

In its practice, critical pedagogy is based on classroom discussion and engaging students in praxis, or the act of moving back and forth between theory, application of theory, and reflection on this application. Students are encouraged to read, think, and talk about societal and cultural structures that might be stifling indigenous or suppressed cultures and those who are otherwise powerless in society (e.g., the poor, women, the disabled, and minority racial and ethnic groups). In a literature classroom, this pedagogy could take the form of reading literary texts about diverse cultures and situations, perhaps far removed from the students' own communities (or, alternately, closely reflecting an unjust community in which they may live). From this literary reading and subsequent response and discussion, students may be enlightened as to pervasive ideologies that affect and influence their daily lives as well as the lives of others and, consequently, could be moved to action.

Connections between critical pedagogy and the experience of identification

As can be extrapolated from the discussion above, reading and responding to literature through a critical frame would entail some ability or desire to identify with characters, settings, or events in a book. One branch of critical theory itself was born in literary study, as it is connected to postmodern and Marxist literary criticism, as a way of interpreting literature not simply as texts that can be understood through close reading and historical study, but as texts that reflect and affect the diverse, varied, and troubled world in which we all live. While complex literary identification as described in this chapter is surely not the only way critical theory becomes critical pedagogy, it is one way young readers might begin to see the holes in the political and cultural milieu in which they live and act.

Returning to the visual model representing the process of literary identification that I supplied earlier in this chapter, it is clear that it necessitates recursive interaction between the text, the reader, and the characters in the fictional work. True identification does not move "one way," in that a book's characters are not mindlessly imitated by the mature reader, nor does this reader quickly and unceremoniously reject characters as "not like me." The true identification process is more complex and can be encouraged and supported through critical theories as transformed into critical pedagogical approaches, strategies, activities and related reading selections. As identification often leads to empathy, it can help young readers see themselves as part of a global network of individuals, all with their own different, yet similar, struggles, together striving for a better world.

BOX 2.1 SAMPLE LITERATURE LESSON TO ENCOURAGE IDENTIFICATION

Contributed by Jeff Spanke, Purdue University, formerly North Montgomery High School, Crawfordsville, Indiana.

"My Blank World"

So far this trimester, we've discussed and read about several different conceptions of the world in narrative texts such as Shakespeare's *Romeo and Juliet,* Angela Johnson's *The First Part Last,* Sandra Cisneros' *The House on Mango Street,* and Sophocles' *Antigone.* We've read how, throughout history, people have made various attempts to try and figure out their world through art, music, film and written text. Some people view the world as a happy, peaceful place full of hope and love, while others consider it a dark, lonely place where people are basically animals. For this assignment, you will write an essay describing your perception of the "world" in which you live.

1. First, think of three to five adjectives that best describe our world. For example, you could say our world is big, wet and hot.
2. Once you have the parameters (your guiding adjectives), you will need to do some research. You will need to find famous quotes, stories, facts, historical narratives, films, movies: anything at all having to do with each adjective. So if you think the world is wet, you could discuss the movie *Waterworld,* use Stephen Crane's "The Open Boat," or look at Prince's *Purple Rain* for analysis. (Note: every adjective must be linked to a source from another country, other than the US.)
3. Using all your research as support, write an essay describing how each adjective combines to paint a picture of our world. *The purpose is to discover how your views of the world compare with those of people who have come before you, or who are living and working right now. Hopefully, you will discover that your views may not be all that different from those of other people all over the world.* Your essay will be a mix of summary, analysis, personal reflection and prediction.

As you conclude your essay, make predictions about the future of our world, based on the literature you've read, the research you've compiled, and the analysis you've done. What will our world look like in 100 years? What forces are behind this movement? Should we stop it? Can we stop it?

References

Alsup, J. (2013). Teaching literature in an age of text complexity. *Journal of Adolescent and Adult Literacy, 57* (3), 181–184.

Apple, M. (1996). *Cultural politics and education.* New York: Teachers College Press.

Bley, E.S. (1945). Identification: A key to literature. *The English Journal, 34* (1), 26–32.

Flood, J., Lapp, D., Squire, J.R. & Jensen, J.M. (Eds) (2003). *Handbook of research on teaching the English language arts.* Mahwah, NJ: Lawrence Erlbaum.

Freire, P. (1968/2000). *The pedagogy of the oppressed, 30th anniversary edition.* London: Bloomsbury Academic Press.

Freud, S. (1925). On narcissism: An introduction. In *Collected Papers, Vol. IV* (pp. 30–59). London: Hogarth.

Gaimon, N. (2013). Why our future depends on libraries, reading and daydreaming. *The Guardian,* October, p. 9. Retrieved from www.theguardian.com/books/2013/oct/15/neil-gaiman-future-libraries-reading-daydreaming

Gallese, V. & Goldman, A. (1998). Mirror neurons and the simulation theory of mind-reading. *Trends in Cognitive Sciences, 2,* 493–501.

Gerrig, R. (1993). *Experiencing narrative worlds: On the psychological activities of reading.* New Haven, CT: Yale University Press.

Giroux, H. (1981). *Ideology, Culture and the Process of Schooling.* Philadelphia, PA: Temple University Press.

Holland, N. (1968/1975). *The dynamics of literary response.* New York: W.W. Norton and Company.

hooks, b. (1994). *Teaching to transgress: Education as the practice of freedom.* New York: Routledge.

hooks, b. (2003). *Teaching community: A pedagogy of hope.* New York: Routledge.

Iacoboni, M. (2008). *Mirroring people: The science of empathy and how we connect with others.* New York: Picador.

Iacoboni, M. (2005). Neural mechanisms of imitation. *Current Opinion in Neurobiology,* 15, 632–637.

Jaén, I. & Simon, J.J. (2012). An overview of recent developments in cognitive literary studies. In I. Jaén and J.J. Simon (Eds), *Cognitive literary studies: Current themes and new directions* (pp. 13–32). Austin, TX: University of Texas Press.

Kidd, D.C. & Castano, E. (2013). Reading literary fiction improves theory of mind. *Science Express.* Retrieved from www.sciencemag.org/content/early/recent (accessed 12/12/2014).

Lewis, C.S. (1952/2002). On three ways of writing for children. In C.S. Lewis, *On stories: And other essays on literature* (pp. 31–44). New York: Mariner Books.

Mar, R.A. & Oatley, K. (2008). The function of fiction is the abstraction and simulation of social experience. *Perspectives on Psychological Science,* 3 (3), 173–192.

McLaren, P. (1995). *Critical pedagogy and predatory culture.* New York: Routledge.

Mead, R. (2014) The scourge of "relatability." *The New Yorker,* August 1.

Nell, V. (1988). *Lost in a book.* New Haven, CT: Yale University Press.

Nelms, B. (Ed.). (1988). *Literature in the classroom: Readers, texts and contexts.* Urbana, NCTE.

Richter, T., Appel, M. & Calio, F. (2014). Stories can change the self-concept. *Social Influence,* 9, 172–188.

Rizzolatti, G. & Craighero, L. (2004). The mirror-neuron system. *Annual Review of Neuroscience,* 27, 169–192.

Rosenblatt, L. (1938/1983). *Literature as exploration,* 4th edn. New York: MLA.

Rosenblatt, L. (1938/1978). *The reader, the text, the poem: The transactional theory of the literary work.* Carbondale: Southern Illinois University Press.

Russell, D.H. & Shrodes, C. (1950). Contributions of research in bibliotherapy to the language-arts program. *The School Review,* 58 (6), 335–342.

Russell, D. (1949). Identification through literature. *Childhood Education,* 25 (9), 397–401.

Shor, I. (1980). *Critical teaching and everyday life.* Chicago: University of Chicago Press.

Thompson, H. (2010). We feel your pain: Extreme Empaths. *New Scientist,* 2751, unpaged.

Woodward, G. (2003). *The idea of identification.* New York: SUNY Press.

Zunshine, L. (2006). *Why we read fiction: Theory of mind and the novel.* Columbus, OH: Ohio State University Press.

3

LITERATURE AND EMPATHY

How Narrative Stimulates Emotion

> Empathy may be uniquely well suited for bridging the gap between egoism and altruism, since it has the property of transforming another person's misfortune into one's own feeling of distress.
>
> *(Hoffman, M.L., 1981, p. 133)*

Empathy seems to be the central topic of interest when reasons for teaching and reading literature are bandied about. Ask many teachers, or many readers, why they think reading narrative fiction is important, and you are bound to hear something like, "because it makes you a better person" or "it helps you understand others unlike yourself." What they are talking about is the development of empathy, or the ability to feel the feelings of others, or to take the perspective of others. Many people seem to believe that reading fiction makes you more deeply understand others, and that such sustained narrative experience has little substitute other than real-world experience, and sometimes that isn't even as powerful. In other words, living in and through a "narrative world" (Gerrig, 1993) is one of the ways human beings become more human.

Even our President seems to agree. In July of 2007, then Senator Obama gave a speech in which he lauded the potential of books to change readers, to enable them to see outside of themselves. He said, in part:

> And the great power of books is the capacity to take you out of yourself and put you somewhere else. And to suddenly say, "Oh, this is what it's like" – maybe not perfectly – but it gives you some glimpse of "This is what it is like to be a woman", or "This is what it is like to be an African-American". Or "This is what it is like to be impoverished in India". Or "This is what it's like to be in the midst of war."
>
> *(Obama, 2007, Literacy and Empathy,*
> *www.youtube.com/watch?v=LGHbbJ5xz3g)*

In fact, there is a website devoted to tracking Obama's speeches (the "Obama empathy speech index") in which he mentions or discusses empathy and what he has labeled the "empathy deficit," or the inability of others to "put themselves in others' shoes" and see the world as they see it (http://cultureofempathy.com/Obama/SpeechIndex.htm). Many, including me, may argue that Obama's sense of literary empathy is oversimplified and potentially colonialist; however, on the flip side, it is refreshing to see a government leader value reading for more than how it can produce higher standardized test scores. If only this ideology were reflected in his administration's educational policy, as its current approaches seem to favor nonfiction texts and narrowly defined definitions of reading, comprehension and response (see National Governors Association, 2012).

Literature teachers, avid readers, and our President are not the only people who believe in the power of literary reading to change readers, to make them more understanding of others' plights. There have been multiple theorists of reading and reader response who have valued the subjective, the personal response over the more distanced, critical one. I've previously mentioned Louise Rosenblatt, whose aesthetic response to a text includes a personal response prior to a critical one. Additionally, "subjective" critics, David Bleich and Norman Holland both assert, like Rosenblatt, that reading is, in its essence, a transaction, and there are as many valid textual interpretations as there are readers. While Holland (1975) still values the text as an objective entity that affects or influences a reader to explore his or her identity themes through a textual mediator, Bleich (1978) sees the reader's part of the transaction as far more important than that of the text, to the point that he asserts that there is no meaning whatsoever in a text without the reader's response and interpretation. While the emphasis these theorists place on the reader in the reader–text transaction may seem extreme, one must remember that they were reacting to the previously unquestioned assumption by the so-called "new critics" that all meaning was in the text, and the text held an objective meaning that could be determined through close reading and analysis. Today, it could be argued that theorists of reader response and teachers of literature have moved more to the middle of the spectrum, as schools of criticism as diverse as feminism, new historicism, disability studies, and critical race studies have tended to value both the text through close reading as well as the subjectivity of the reader.

Regardless of where you stand on the reader-response spectrum, there are several potential problems with the theory that reading literature produces empathy and changes a reader's response to others (despite the growing body of empirical evidence linking reading and self-reports of empathetic response, which I will summarize later in this chapter). One possible problem with the assumption that reading narrative fiction results in empathetic feeling is that there are actually completely nice people who don't like to read fiction, and read fictional narratives very rarely. How can they be caring people and not be readers of fiction? How can they possibly "walk in another's shoes" as advocated by President Obama, if they have not been lost in a narrative world? And on the flip side, there are terribly mean people who like to read novels. How do we explain them? Second, while there is a large body of existing evidence thinking feelings of empathy and altruistic behavior, and linking reading literary fiction with feelings of empathy, there is little research connecting reading literature to prosocial, altruistic behavior. So while we may be able to say with little reasonable doubt that fiction readers tend to be more empathetic (either fiction makes them that way, or they are drawn to fiction because of their empathetic nature), and people who express empathy tend to engage in more helping behavior, there has been little empirical evidence supporting the intuitive assumption that readers are better people (Keen, 2006, p. 208). I have been able to find only one study that makes a firm connection between reading narrative fiction and helping behavior, which I will discuss in Chapter 5.

English teachers probably revert to the empathy argument for the teaching of literature more than any other group because we are ourselves readers of fiction, and we have experienced emotional response to it first hand, many times. We know experientially, anecdotally and intuitively that something happens to you when reading a novel—when that "flow" experience takes over and you forget surroundings, time, obligations, worries, commitments, all because you are living in a narrative world for that short time. We know that we emerge different. But we must remember that not everyone has had such experience or believes in the veracity of such an experience, and it seems that those who have experienced it are becoming fewer and fewer. And, despite President Obama's apparent advocacy for reading and literary study, his Common Core State Standards arguably undermine the teaching of literature at the expense of informational, non-narrative texts that are seen to be more complex and demanding of young readers.

Assuming that empathy is enhanced by reading, or that better empathizers are better readers, why would readers come to a text that might take them through a difficult emotional experience, one that is not their own, one that they wouldn't have to experience? What makes readers choose to live through an emotional experience, not their own, which might be difficult and painful, when it's a choice (assuming that the book has not been assigned by a teacher)? Why not just close the book—or not begin it at all? What about the experience is pleasurable, or useful, or worth seeking out?

Various theorists and researchers have answered this question in a number of ways: Gerrig (1993) and Nell (1988) describe a sort of pleasurable "flow" experience; (Csikszentmihalyi, 1990), Rosenblatt (1965/1995), Holland (1975), Rorty (1989) and Bleich (1978) argue that such reading helps develop the self; Nussbaum (1997) and Bloom (2000) argue that reading results in enhanced cultural awareness or global citizenship; and Keen (2006, 2007) and Zunshine (2006) argue that fiction provides a space for readers to work out their responses to others and practice "mind reading" in a safe, unreal world. And, of course, over two thousand years ago, Aristotle argued that catharsis, through drama and literary experience, could cleanse a person of potentially poisonous emotions (*Poetics*, 335 BCE/1997).

To complicate the issue even further, readers who regularly identify with characters and events in fictional texts don't all respond to the same texts in the same ways. Some readers might respond emotionally to one text, while others may remain untouched. Why do I cry at the end of Applegate's (2013) *The One and Only Ivan* while another reader is simply annoyed and bored at the idea of a gorilla with feelings and the motivation to help another? The obvious answer, I think, hearkens back to the subjective reader response theorists who argue for the primacy of the reader's experience in the reading transaction: we are all different, we all have had different experiences, hence we react differently to narrative worlds. So are there any generalizations at all that we can make about readers and their empathetic experiences with stories? And, if so, are these generalizations helpful or useful to teachers and teacher educators? Researchers have begun to explore these questions as I will discuss below, but answers are far from definitive.

Regardless, narratives have seemed to have a pragmatic function throughout human evolution—stories around a campfire warn of dangers, and fairy stories and nursery rhymes clearly have a teaching function to keep children away from harmful situations by evoking fear. Even in the present day, friends often tell friends stories of mistakes or failures as a kind of warning, or cautionary tale. Often, stories inspire emotions parallel to empathy: fear, tension, nervousness, uneasiness, and laughter. It seems clear there is evolutionary significance to narratives, as I mentioned in the introductory chapter.

The question that pervades this chapter is to what extent can we continue to use the empathy argument as a viable one for the teaching of literature in secondary schools? And, if that argument is viable, how do we best, and most persuasively, make it?

What is Empathy?

Empathy is most often defined as the vicarious, often visceral and spontaneous, expression of emotion in response to witnessing another's emotional state (Keen, 2006). Scholars in various fields, including psychology, philosophy, and biological science, define empathy, and the definitions are applied to research in those disparate fields. Professor of Primate Behavior, Frans B.M. de Waal, defines empathy as "the capacity to (a) be affected by and share the emotional state of another, (b) assess the reasons for the other's state, and (c) identify with the other, adopting his or her perspective" (2008, p. 281).

The English word "empathy" has been around a surprisingly short amount of time. It first appeared in 1909 in the work of American psychologist Edward B. Titchener as he translated the German version of the word, proposed by philosopher Theodor Lipps at the end of the 19th century (Dolby, 2012, p. 47). One key idea about empathy is that it differs from sympathy, which is defined by Eisenberg (2000) as "an affective response that consists of feelings of sorrow or concern for a distressed or needy other (rather than sharing the emotion of the other)" (p. 677). According to most theorists, including F.B.M. de Waal, there are several different types (or levels) of empathy, notably:

1 *emotional contagion*, or the base, physical and/or emotional response of one in response to another (e.g., one baby crying makes others cry);
2 *sympathetic, affective concern*, or emotional contagion as combined with some, small cognitive attempt to understand another's perspective or context;
3 *perspective taking*, which is a more cognitively driven enterprise in which one being attempts to adopt another's point of view and imagine what life would be like as them;
4 *narrative empathy*, as explored by Suzanne Keen and Lisa Zunshine, among others, who discuss the role of narrative fiction in the development of theory of mind or the ability to better understand the emotions and motives of others.

In the sections that follow, I outline some of the major components and theories of empathy as defined by leading empathy scholars, and I end by investigating the concept of narrative empathy, which is really what this chapter, and perhaps this book, is about.

Animal emotion

A couple of weeks ago, I attended a lecture by Frans B.M. de Waal (2014) about empathy in primates. He made the point that in his primate research, empathy seems to be more strongly felt toward those similar to the empathizer—in appearance, family structure, role in the group, etc. Another interesting thing mentioned by de Waal was the notion of a "self–other distinction" as being central to primate empathy. Primates who in mirror tests were able to recognize themselves in the mirror's reflection, and were, therefore, able to distinguish their own self from others were more apt to engage in helping behaviors toward others. In other words, they had to recognize their own individuality, and the individuality of others, to be moved to help another.

If one can make the leap from gorillas, bonobos, and chimpanzees to humans, it could be assumed that two things might be the case, based on de Waal's comments: people (readers) may empathize more strongly and easily with others (characters) who are like them; people (readers) who have a better sense of self and can differentiate between their own needs/desires/problems and those of others might be more ready empathizers. If this argument can be applied to human readers, even young adult readers, it may be an argument for using literature with more immature readers containing characters and settings reflective of their own lives; then, as adolescents develop and grow cognitively and emotionally, they might be presented with texts that ask them to stretch their empathy muscles and connect with characters and settings less and less like those readily familiar. As readers mature and identities develop, it becomes easier for them to both differentiate themselves from the characters about whom they read, and connect (or identify) with them in more complex, more subtle, and less obvious ways. As I stated at the end of the previous chapter, identification can be a stepping-stone for feelings of empathy.

While such leaps between primate expressions of empathy and human empathetic response may be stretching de Waal's research into areas he never intended, his research, and the research of others on animal emotion, may lead us to some interesting hypotheses about human feelings of empathy and what conditions might inspire it to be felt the strongest.

Simulation theories of empathy

One theory that is popular to explain how and why reading fiction might affect empathy is the "simulation" theory of empathy. This theory, offered most visibly by Canadian researchers Raymond Mar and Keith Oatley, asserts that fictional narratives "offer models or simulations of the social world via abstraction, simplification, and compression" (2008, p. 173). They argue that "engaging in the simulative experiences of fiction literature can facilitate the understanding of others who are different from ourselves and can augment our capacity for empathy and social inference" (p. 173).

Simulations are used in many fields to find answers to burning questions, including the sciences and technology. In the field of empathy studies, simulations are seen to have similar purposes: both as models to help explain behavior or phenomenon, and as a way to predict future behavior in similar situations or environments and respond appropriately (Mar & Oatley, p. 175). In both cases, simulations involve making abstractions of real life experience. The same can be argued for a fictional text, as it is an abstraction of sorts of real experience; it's not real, but it is a sort of composite of various imagined and experienced events translated by the author for reader consumption. Fiction is a sort of alternate reality, or virtual reality that allows trial and experimentation with low risk of failure or dealing with negative consequences. Mar and Oatley hypothesize that such simulated fictional experiences can lead to greater empathy toward others, even though the experience of the reader is highly mediated by a text which is only an abstraction of real experience (p. 181). In fact, they argue, similar to Keen (2006) that fiction might actually be *more* effective in stimulating empathy because it allows a safe space for trial and error. Reading researcher Jèmeljan Hakemulder (2000), borrowing from Gardner (1978), went so far as to call reading fiction a "moral laboratory," in which a reader can observe and learn from a narrative's characters and events—without experiencing any real-life effects (p. 13).

One additional thought is about how the simulation theory of reading and response might relate to imitation. Meltzoff and Decety argue that infant imitation is a foundation for the development of empathy and theory of mind in adults (2014, p. 491). As I discussed in the previous section about animal empathy, it seems that emotional contagion, the simplest level of empathy, mostly comprises imitation: people (or animals) feel parallel emotions to someone or something they are watching; in other words, when you see someone take a bad fall and experience pain, you might yourself grimace or shout out, as if you were experiencing the same physical pain yourself. If you see someone yawn, you yourself yawn. It could be possible that emotional contagion, or imitation, happens with younger adolescent readers after identification with a character or series of events in a text, particularly if the character is like them in age, appearance, or lifestyle and the events of the narrative are similar to their own experiences. This might explain why young adult literature often results in more behavioral imitation than when adults read so-called adult books, particularly in the younger grades. For example, I have had college students tell me that they remember dressing up like Harry Potter or Hermione, imitating the behavior of the mean girls in the series *The Clique*, or having an increased interest in learning archery after reading *The Hunger Games*. I can't remember the last time I heard an adult reader of an adult book discuss dressing like or imitating a main character. If this hypothesis is true, it might change how teachers in the middle grades approach book selection or how they conceptualize literary discussions and response.

Narrative empathy

> Most clinical and counseling psychologists, however, agree that true empathy requires three distinct skills: the ability to share the other person's feelings, the cognitive ability to intuit what another person is feeling, and a "socially beneficial" intention to respond compassionately to that person's distress.
>
> *(Hatfield et al., in press)*

Interestingly, this definition assumes that the empathizer can engage in several so-called levels of empathy: emotional contagion, perspective taking, and helping behavior, or prosocial action. I've discovered one definition of empathy that bridges the gap between the knee-jerk emotional contagion and the imaginative, cognitive theory of mind. This type of empathy may just be narrative empathy, or a type of empathy that results when a human reader experiences a fictional, narrative text.

Narrative empathy seems to involve both emotional or affective empathy and more cognitive, or imaginative empathy, such as what happens during perspective taking. Narrative empathy might manifest itself in a bodily response, such as a raise in blood pressure or sweaty palms, and, alternatively, in a quite sophisticated intellectual response (e.g., if I were Romeo, I could have changed my fate by being less impulsive). Such feelings of empathy as a response to reading fiction narrative are often addressed under the heading Theory of Mind, defined by Leverage, Mancing, Schweickert, and William (2011) as "mind reading, empathy, creative imagination of another's perspective: in short, it is simultaneously a highly sophisticated ability, and a very basic necessity for human communication" (p. 1). Lisa Zunshine (2006) takes the argument a step further by asserting that not only does theory of mind get piqued during reading fiction, but theory of mind is a motivation for humans to read because reading actually improves one's theory of mind, thereby improving how one interacts with others and one's social success (p. 10). Interestingly, the first coinage of theory of mind was in the context of studies with chimpanzees, when researchers determined a chimp named Sarah was exhibiting helpful intentions to a human being displaying a problem (Leverage, et al. 2011, p. 3). So humans may not be the only primates to display theory of mind, although we might be alone in our ability to experience it through the reading of fiction.

Another interesting aspect of narrative empathy involves various theories of narrative structures or devices that seem to increase the empathetic responses of readers, for example, first person narration, the representation of characters' internal thoughts through monologues, and the inclusion of a character with whom readers can readily identify (Keen, 2006). In the section below about research into narrative empathy, I will share more details about what narrative structures, literary devices, and stylistic moves have been associated with empathetic response of readers.

Below I have included a visual image of a theory of how the various levels of empathetic response might be connected to the concept of narrative empathy, which is called Narrative Context in the figure. While it is not a given that all types of empathy must be felt by the reader for any empathetic response to result during a reading process, it is arguable that the narrative context providing the opportunity for narrative empathy to result (and increased theory of mind) might in the ideal reading experience involve each level as the reader identifies with characters emotionally and maybe bodily (emotional contagion), experiences an emotional response to a character and/or situation that is built on some level of understanding the fictional experience and perhaps even sympathizing with the character(s) (affective empathy), and is led to imagine him or herself in the shoes of a character and consider how he or she might respond in a similar situation (perspective taking). The narrative itself, or the narrative context, allows, and perhaps prompts, each and all of these responses to occur in the reader. Of course, what is missing in this figure is what I alluded to at the beginning of this chapter: how does all this feeling as stimulated by literary reading affect real-life behavior? Does narrative empathy affect how readers act in the real world, beyond simple imitation?

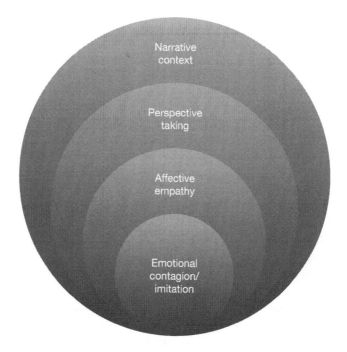

FIGURE 3.1 Levels of empathetic response. This figure is derived from Frans B.M. de Waal's "Russian doll model" of empathy in primates, in which higher cognitive levels of empathy are built upon more "hard wired" emotional responses (de Waal, 2008, p. 287).

The Affective Fallacy and Other Problems with Empathy

I wrote briefly earlier in this chapter about some problems or questions related to understanding the relationship between empathy and reading, notably the fact that not all empathetic people are readers, and readers tend to react quite differently to texts based on their own memories and experiences. I'd like to address three additional arguments problematizing the idea of narrative empathy, namely the so-called affective fallacy, immoral or unethical empathy, and the possible promotion of censorship.

The term 'affective fallacy' was coined by Beardsley and Wimsatt (1971) in the late '40s and early '50s. As proponents of the New Criticism, they believed it was a grave error to judge a work of literature based on the emotional effect it has on readers. This was a clear difference in opinion from the subjective critics, whom I discussed earlier, who followed them. Judging a text based primarily on how it made a reader feel, such as empathy, would simply result in emotional relativism and the disregard of the importance of the text as an object with inherent, objective meaning. Of course, to us today, surrounded by post-postmodern criticism and social/cultural analyses of texts, such an approach sounds absurd.

However, the idea is still powerful with some who believe that a text should be judged on its own merits, as determined through primarily text-based, unemotional criticism.

Second, when readers empathize with a narrative and its characters or events, they often begin by identifying with these characters or events. This process of identification can vary, according to the age and sophistication of the reader, as I discussed in the previous chapter. Therefore, it's possible that this identification, this empathizing, can be reductive and even stereotypical, what Keen calls "empathic inaccuracy" (2006, p. 222). Even worse, some theorists (Keen, 2006, 2007; Williams, 1958) argue that feeling empathy in response to a text might even forestall, and replace, feelings of real empathy that could lead to social action, something Keen calls amoral empathy (2006, p. 222). Either way, the empathic reaction to a text, toward or for a text's characters or events, might not always be positive or prosocial. In fact, it may result in misunderstandings of others, incorrect or discriminatory beliefs, and a failure to act in real life. Jurecic (2011) writes, empathic responses to texts might not only be authentic stimulants for social action, but also "expressions of power, appropriations of others' experience, and falsely oversimplified understandings of social and cultural relationships" (p. 11). She argues that such harmful responses can be tempered through classroom teaching of literature that recognizes the complexity of narrative empathy and literary identification and scaffolds students as they progress emotionally through a text, allowing them opportunity to both relate and question, compare and consider possibilities— something she calls "suspicious criticism" (p. 16).

Last, but certainly not least in importance, is the notion, or problem, of censorship. According to the idea of narrative empathy, you have the text, a work of fiction that is mediating the identification/empathy process for a reader. The text is in-between the reader and the response, working reciprocally with the reader, sparking identification and then leading to empathic response of various forms, both emotional and cognitive. However, narrative empathy is always tempered by the text, which sits in-between, a substitute or simulation for, or abstraction of, the real-life person or experience depicted. Therefore, the text can readily be given credit (or blamed) for creating a certain emotional response or disposition in a reader. This seems to happen most often with children's or young adult literature, as adult readers are often trusted with being aware of the difference between fact and fiction, and being able to impede behavior responses to fictional events. However, children and young adults are often not given this consideration, and adults can worry about how a young reader might imitate narrative behaviors or even assume the point of view of a fictional character.

When we write and talk about narrative empathy and theory of mind, I think it's especially important to be wary of steering close to a censorship argument. Simply because literature is emotionally powerful, doesn't mean readers are thoughtlessly influenced by it to engage in risky behaviors or anti-social decision-making. When these things do happen, there is usually more to the story than just reading.

Researching Empathy

There has been much research in the last ten to fifteen years exploring connections between reading literature and readers' feelings of empathy. A great deal of this research will cite studies in the 1980s and 1990s of Di Pellegrino et al. (1992), Gallese et al. (1996), and Rizzolatti et al. (1996) about the discovery of mirror neurons, a "particular class of visuomotor neurons, originally discovered in area F5 of the monkey premotor cortex, that discharge both when the monkey does a particular action and when it observes another individual (monkey or human) doing a similar action" (Rizzolatti & Craighero, 2004, p. 169). While some neuroscientists dispute the existence of mirror neurons altogether (Dinstein et al., 2008), their existence as argued by other scientists has inspired many psychologists, narratologists, and literary scholars who use the existence of mirror neurons as support for theorized connections between reading fiction and developing an enhanced theory of mind, or the ability to understand others. The argument goes, that if seeing a behavior or action can create a similar neurological response in a viewer, why can't reading fiction, and internally imaging events and characters, result in similar, parallel responses in readers? To extend the argument, why can't reading fiction inspire empathy and emotion in a reader that just might transfer into real-life settings?

In what follows, I briefly review the literature exploring this question, sorting it into summaries, or a meta-analysis of studies of cognition, reading and emotion; empirical research studies which demonstrate measurable connections between reading and empathy; and studies which discuss how the foregrounding of various narrative techniques in fiction differently affect the empathic responses of readers.

First, I address the summaries or meta-narratives. In 1995, David S. Miall, a leading Canadian researcher on literature and cognition, published a lengthy description of existing research on literary reading and the brain. Citing research conducted by neuroscientists, reader response theorists, literary scholars, and psychologists, Miall concludes that "feelings appear to play a central role in initiating and directing the interpretive activities involved in such complex activities as reading" (Miall, 1995, p. 1). He pays particular attention to research that explores anticipation in literary reading and how that influences reader response (Olson et al., 1981; Hobbs, 1990; Simon, 1994) and how the foregrounding of various literary features in a narrative text changes reader response, studies I will summarize later in this section. At the end of his lengthy synthesis of research, Miall argues for continued multi-disciplinary research empirically investigating the social and cultural effects of reading.

A second meta-narrative is one by Immordino-Yang and Damasio (2007) which argues, through a review of research, that "emotion related processes are required for skills and knowledge to be transferred from the structured school environment to real-world decision making because they provide an *emotional rudder* to guide judgment and action" (p. 3). They go on to argue that many aspects of human life, including culture, morality, and creativity, can be explained, in part, with neurobiology (p. 3). Citing researchers in psychology and education (Gardner et al., 2001; Damasio, 1994), the authors argue that emotion is central to ethical decision-making, learning, attention, motivation, and memory (p. 7).

Moving to research, which more specifically addresses the role of literature in the emotional response, I'll begin with a study published by Djikic et al. (2009) which tested the hypothesis that reading a literary text will affect personality, as mediated by emotion, more than a documentary version of the same material. They discovered that readers of a Chekhov story experienced more personality change as measured on an "emotion checklist" than those who read a factual discussion of the same series of events. They conclude, "if fiction can produce fluctuations in one's own traits ... it seems reasonable to assume that this process can casually lead to a gradual change of oneself toward a better understanding of others as well" (p. 28).

Similarly, Mar et al. (2009) conducted a study to determine if reading fiction could predict a certain performance on a empathy task; they wanted to rule out the possibility which arose during an earlier study (Mar et al., 2006) that individual personality traits were the cause for connection between reading and measures of empathy, not the reading experience itself. They discovered that even when statistically controlling for personality variables, "fiction exposure still predicted performance on an empathy task" [including surveys and interpretations of actors' emotions by looking at photos of their eyes] while "exposure to nonfiction, in contrast, was associated with loneliness" (p. 407). They conclude by stating that this study confirms their 2006 results showing that reading fiction can have a great effect on a reader's emotional life.

In 1993, Bourg et al. studied 6th graders' inference-making related to narrative texts and the effect of explicit teacher instruction in empathy-building on the quality of these inferences. They found that when students participated in a guided empathy-building strategy asking them to take on the perspectives of fictional characters they were more successful in making inferences about the text, particularly when the text contained a large number of "causal connections" (p. 117). This study sheds light on the importance of teachers in literature study by suggesting that explicit instruction and practice in perspective taking can lead to a deeper understanding of a story. Similar findings were reported by Golden and Guthrie (1986) who found that empathizing with story characters was associated with how 9th graders interpreted the theme of a text (pp. 248–249) and by Phillips (1988) who found that empathizing with characters was one of the strategies that differentiated good from poor readers (p. 205).

Last, I'd like to return to the issue of "foregrounding" (Mukarovsky, 1932/1964) features of narrative text, such as imagery, figurative language, symbolism, rhyme, and point of view, and how they might affect the empathic responses of readers.

Earlier, I mentioned the work of Keen (2006) who speculates about the importance of foregrounding for deep reader response. Additionally, there are multiple research studies that support her point of view, concluding that such features that tend to mark "literary" texts as different from normal, everyday language, cause readers to slow down and attend to a text more carefully, hence resulting in a deeper response. While there is disagreement on many fronts about what actually constitutes a "literary" versus a "nonliterary" text, the research about narrative empathy seems to suggest that a deeper empathetic response results from texts that contain more foregrounded features that surprise the reader and "defamiliarize" the text for him or her (Miall, 2006, p. 113), leading to greater attention and emotional response.

Miall and Kuiken (1994) conducted a study with short fiction in which they asked readers to read the stories twice, the second time rating them for "feeling, strikingness, importance, or discussion value" (quoted in Miall, 2006 p. 112). The amount of foregrounding in each story strongly predicted reading times and ratings for strikingness and feeling (p. 112). Hakemulder (2004) reports on the results of several studies he conducted to explore the effect to which foregrounded textual features affect reader responses. He found that after multiple readings, participants usually responded to original literary texts with much foregrounding of literary devices with stronger aesthetic appreciation and positive responses. His conclusion is that "foregrounding may enhance aesthetic appreciation and may be responsible for effects on perception" (p. 193).

While a link between foregrounded literary elements that can be associated with classic or canonical literature and a stronger emotional response of readers has been demonstrated in several studies, it is possible that other features of the text also contributed to strong reader response, such as content of subject matter, reader preference, and genre. These qualities of so-called "literary" texts remain largely untested, and I believe it would be premature to claim that any one type of text, as defined through stylistic qualities, automatically results in a more power-ful reader response than another. However, the relative power of various types of narrative texts is a question that should continue to be explored in future research.

The Pedagogy of Empathy

Teaching for social justice

Teaching for social justice is a concept that seems particularly well suited to encouraging empathetic responses to fiction. As this approach focuses on fostering an awareness of injustice, unfairness, or inequity in the world and critical analysis of how such injustice might be rectified, it seems that engaging in genuine empathy may be an important precursor to or element within literature pedagogies promoting empathy. In what follows, I first define briefly what teaching for social justice means; then, I connect the concept to the idea of empathy and the processes through which empathy might be encouraged or invited on the part of young readers. Finally, as in Chapter 2, I link teaching literature for social justice to promote empathy to the visual model of empathetic response provided in Figure 3.1.

What is teaching for social justice?

Social justice is a phrase that seems to have grown in popularity in educational circles over the last ten to fifteen years. While discussions with students about societal injustice and unfairness may not be new (one can cite John Dewey [1937/2008] or Paulo Freire [1970] as early social justice advocates), calling such teaching "teaching for social justice" is relatively contemporary. Social justice, in its essence, is fairness and equity, applied to all, regardless of "race, ethnicity, gender, gender expression, age, appearance, ability, national origin, language, spiritual belief, size, sexual orientation, social class, economic circumstance, environment, ecology, culture, and the treatment of animals" ("Beliefs about Social Justice in English Education," 2009, see National Council for Teachers of English website at www.ncte.org/cee/positions/socialjustice). While social justice in education is sometimes a contested concept, as some see it as motivated by liberal politics or too personal and nebulous to actually enact and assess in a classroom, its popularity is undeniable, particularly among scholars of literacy and English education (see Ayers, 1998; DeStigter, 2008; Miller and Norris, 2007; Alsup and Miller, 2014). In fact, in the most recent iteration of the National Council of Teachers of English (NCTE)/Council for the Accreditation of Educator Preparation (CAEP) standards for English teacher education programs, there is an entire standard devoted to how "theories and research of social justice, diversity, equity, student identities, and schools as institutions can enhance students' opportunities to learn in English Language Arts" (www.ncte.org/library/NCTEFiles/Groups/CEE/NCATE/ApprovedStandards_111212.pdf).

Teaching for social justice would incorporate pedagogical techniques and strategies that encourage students to think about social justice in their worlds (or its lack, as the case may be) through critical reflection, discussion, engaged response, or other student-centered practices. Clearly, techniques consistent with a critical pedagogical approach, as discussed in the previous chapter, could be used by a teacher seeking to raise students' awareness of social justice issues through the study of literature. A related way social justice teaching is defined concerns how the teacher him or herself interacts with students on a daily basis: does the teacher recognize individual, diverse student identities and seek to respond to these individualities with appropriate and relevant instruction? Hence, the importance of social justice to teacher education, as most teacher educators strive to encourage the development in new teachers of a professional disposition promoting social justice in the classroom, in all of its forms (Alsup and Miller, 2014).

Connections between teaching for social justice pedagogy and the experience of empathy

Social justice pedagogy, while sometimes talked about in relationship to preparing teachers or thinking about an umbrella teaching disposition or philosophy, could also be used as a guiding principle in teaching literature to adolescents. Empathy, or the expression of emotion in response to another's, seems essential to developing a true sense of social justice, equity and fairness. To believe that social justice is an issue important in society, one must see inequity and unfairness as unacceptable, even if those inequities occur to another and are only noticed or understood vicariously, such as through reading and responding to fiction. Just as in the earlier section I noted that identifying with characters, events or settings might be essential to critical pedagogy, it seems that experiencing empathy for these same characters, events or settings might be an important part of a social justice-inspired classroom. For if a young reader does not see any injustice in the world, or only sees his or her own perceived injustices, there will be no sense of a wider need for activism to promote social justice; without this activist orientation, there is therefore no true social justice teaching.

Returning to the model mentioned earlier in this chapter, it is evident that the "narrative context," or the experience of reading a fictional work, can inspire empathy, first as "emotional contagion," and later as affective empathy or, even more intellectualized, perspective taking. The narrative experience allows such empathy to be experienced by the reader, even if the maturity of the reader might influence the type of empathy felt, and the depth and complexity of empathy may increase as a reader gains more narrative, and worldly, experience. Such empathetic experiences, particularly the higher "levels" such as perspective taking, may assist in the creation of a social justice orientation to the world, amounting to identity shift and possible behavior change.

BOX 3.1 SAMPLE LITERATURE LESSON TO ENCOURAGE EMPATHY

Contributed by Laura Whitcombe, McCutcheon High School, Lafayette, Indiana.

"Journaling about *The House on Mango Street* by Sandra Cisneros"

As you read and respond to the themes and issues in this novel, you will journal about your reactions to the various vignettes. Some of the issues approached in the novel include immigration, rape, domestic violence, the American Dream, poverty, education, race, and gender roles.

First, you will make the physical journal itself; using any kind of paper or artwork you would like, create the writing space where you will reflect on the text. Then, you will react in several ways to the book's vignettes:

Choice 1: Each vignette has rich images, which you may choose to draw.
Choice 2: You may choose to answer the study guide questions provided.
Choice 3: You may choose to respond to the issues explored in that particular vignette by focusing on one of the following "empathy prompts."

Of the forty-four chapters in the novel, you must respond in writing to at least half of them. This allows you to "opt in" when you have something important to contribute, or "opt out" if the topic of the vignette is too personal or will expose something too private.

Prompts that may promote empathy: Here are some writing prompts that may help you identity with or empathize with the novel's characters. These are gathered from many teaching sources; some are revised, and some are original.

- How is your hair connected to your identity? Describe differences in your family members' hair.
- What is Esperanza's "red balloon"? What is your "red balloon"?
- How does Esperanza feel about her name? How do you feel about your name? Why?
- Describe an event where you experienced bigotry in the way that Cathy talks about Esperanza's people.
- How does your language affect your identity?
- Describe a time when you had "locked your doors" or had "doors locked" on you because of your identity.
- Have you ever had an event that started out with shame and turned into pride?
- Why does Esperanza separate herself from her family? Why would you?
- Once you leave home will you ever be able to return? Really?

Post reading: After reading, you will be asked to research and write about one of the themes of the novel more fully in the form of a newspaper article that residents of the novel's neighborhood might read.

References

Alsup, J. & Miller, S.J. (2014). Reclaiming English education: Rooting social justice in dispositions. *English Education*, 46(3), 195–215.

Applegate, K. (2013). *The One and Only Ivan*. Patricia Castelao, illustrator. New York: HarperCollins.

Aristotle (335 BCE/1997). *Poetics (Penguin Classics)*. New York: Penguin Classics.

Ayers, W. (1998). Popular education: Teaching for social justice. In W. Ayers, J.A. Hunt, & T. Quinn (Eds), *Teaching for social justice*, pp. xvi–xxv. New York: The New Press.

Beardsley, M. & Wimsatt, W.K. (1971). The affective fallacy. Reprinted in Hazard Adams (Ed.), *Critical theory since Plato*. New York: Harcourt Brace Jovanovich.

Bleich, D. (1978). *Subjective criticism*. Balitmore, MD: Johns Hopkins University Press.

Bloom, H. (2000). *How to read and why*. New York: Scribner.

Bourg, T., Risden, K., Thompson, S. & Davis, E.C. (1993). The effects of an empathy-building strategy on 6th graders' causal inferencing in narrative text comprehension. *Poetics*, 22, 117–133.

Csikszentmihalyi, M. (1990). *Flow: The psychology of optimal experience*. New York: Harper and Row.

Damasio, A.R. (1994). *Descartes' error: Emotion, reason and the human brain*. New York: Avon Books.

DeStigter, T. (2008). Lifting the veil of ignorance: Thoughts on the future of social justice teaching. In S. Miller, L. Beliveau, T. DeStigter, D. Kirkland, & P. Rice (Eds), *Narratives of social justice teaching: How English teachers negotiate theory and practice between preservice and inservice spaces*, pp. 121–144. New York: Peter Lang.

de Waal, F.B.M. (2008). Putting the altruism back into altruism: The evolution of empathy. *Annual Review of Psychology*, 59, 279–300.

de Waal, F.B.M. (2014). Prosocial primates: Empathy in animals and humans. Lecture conducted from Purdue University, West Lafayette, IN, April 1.

Dewey, J. (1937/2008). Education and social change. In Jo Ann Boydston (Ed.) *The later works of John Dewey, Vol. 11, 1925–1953*. Evansville, IL: SUI Press.

Djikic, M., Oatley, K., Zoeterman, S. & Peterson, J.B. (2009). On being moved by art: How reading fiction transforms the self. *Creativity Research Journal*, 21(1), 24–29.

Dinstein, I., Thomas, C., Behrmann, M. & Heeger, D.J. (2008). A mirror up to nature. *Current Biology*, 18(3), R13–R18.

Di Pellegrino, G., Fadiga, L., Fogassi, L., Gallese, V. & Rizzolatti, G. (1992). Understanding motor events: A neurophysiological study. *Exp. Brain Res.*, 91, 176–180.

Dolby, N. (2012). *Rethinking multicultural education for the next generation*. New York: Routledge.

Eisenberg, N. (2000). Empathy and sympathy. In M. Lewis, & J.M. Haviland-Jones (Eds), *Handbook of Emotion*, 2nd edn, pp. 677–691. New York: Guilford.

Freire, P. (1970). *Pedagogy of the oppressed*. New York: Herder and Herder.

Gallese, V., Fadiga, L., Fogassi, L. & Rizzolatti, G. (1996). Action recognition in the premotor cortex. *Brain*, 119, 593–609.

Gardner, H., Csikszentmihaly, M. & Damon, W. (2001). *Good work: When excellence and ethics meet*. New York: Basic Books.

Gardner, J. (1978). *On moral fiction*. Chicago: Harper Collins.

Gerrig, R. (1993). *Experiencing narrative worlds: On the psychological activities of reading*. New Haven, CT: Yale University Press.

Golden, J.M. & Guthrie, J.T. (1986). Convergence and divergence in reader response to literature. *Reading Research Quarterly*, 21(4), 408–421.

Hakemulder, J. (2000). *The moral laboratory: Experiments examining the effects of reading literature on social perception and moral self-concept*. Amsterdam and Philadelphia, PA: John Benjamins.

Hakemulder, J.F. (2004). Foregrounding and its effect on readers' perception. *Discourse Processes*, 38(2), 193–218.

Hatfield, E., Rapson, R.L., & Le, Y.L. (in press). Primitive emotional contagion: Recent research. In J. Decety and W. Ickes, (Eds), *The social neuroscience of empathy*. Boston, MA: MIT Press.

Hobbs, J.R. (1990). *Literature and cognition*. Stanford: Center for the Study of Language and Information.

Hoffman, M.L. (1981). Is altruism part of human nature? *Journal of Personality and Social Psychology*, 40(1), 121–137.

Holland, N.N. (1975). *5 Readers Reading*. New Haven, CT: Yale University Press.

Immordino-Yang, M.H. & Damasio, A. (2007). We feel, therefore we learn: The relevance of affective and social neuroscience to education. *Mind Brain and Education*, 1(1), 3–10.

Jurecic, A. (2011). Empathy and the critic. *College English*, 74(1), 10–27.

Keen, S. (2007). *Empathy and the novel*. New York: Oxford University Press.

Keen, S. (2006). A theory of narrative empathy. *Narrative*, 14(3), 207–236.

Leverage, P., Mancing, H., Schweickert, R. & William, J.M. (Eds) (2011). *Theory of mind and literature*. West Lafayette, IN: Purdue University Press.

Mar, R.A., Oatley, K., Hirsh, J., dela Paz, J. & Peterson, J.B. (2006). Bookworms versus nerds: Exposure to fiction versus nonfiction, divergent associations with social ability, and the simulation of fictional social worlds. *Journal of Research in Personality*, 40, 694–712.

Mar, R.A. & Oatley, K. (2008). The function of fiction is the abstraction and simulation of social experience. *Perspectives on Psychological Science*, 3(3), 173–192.

Mar, R.A., Oatley, K. & Peterson, J.B. (2009). Exploring the link between reading fiction and empathy: Ruling out individual differences and examining outcomes. *Communications*, 34, 407–428.

Meltzoff, A.N. & Decety, J. (2014). What imitation tells us about social cognition: A rapprochement between developmental psychology and cognitive neuroscience. *Philosophical Transactions: Biological Sciences*, 358(1431), 491–500.

Miall, D.S. (1995). Anticipation and feeling in literary response. *Poetics,* 23, 275–298.

Miall, D.S. (2006). *Literary reading: Empirical and theoretical studies*. New York: Peter Lang.

Miall, D.S. & Kuiken, D. (1994). Foregrounding, defamiliarization, and affect: Response to literary stories. *Poetics,* 22, 389–407.

Miller, S.J & Norris, L. (2007). *Unpacking the loaded teacher matrix: Negotiating space and time between university and secondary English classrooms*. New York: Peter Lang.

Mukarovsky (1932/1964). Standard language and poetic language. In P.L. Garvin (Ed.), *A Prague school reader on esthetics, literary structure, and style* (pp. 17–30). Washington, DC: Georgetown University Press.

National Governors Association Center for Best Practices & Council of Chief State School Officers (2012). *Appendix A: New Research on Text Complexity*. Washington, DC: Authors. Retrieved from www.corestandards.org/wp-content/uploads/E0813_Appendix_A_New_Research_on_Text_Complexity.pdf

Nell, V. (1988). *Lost in a book*. New Haven, CT: Yale University Press.

Nussbaum, M.C. (1997). *Cultivating humanity: A classical defense of reform in liberal education*. Cambridge, MA: Harvard University Press.

Obama Empathy Speech Index. Retrieved from http://cultureofempathy.com/Obama/SpeechIndex.htm

Obama, B. (2007). Obama, Literacy and Empathy. Retrieved from http://youtube.com/watch?v=LGHbbJ5xz3g

Olson, G.M., Mack, R.L. & Duffy, S.A. (1981). Cognitive aspects of genre. *Poetics*, 10, 183–315.

Phillips, L.M. (1988). Young readers' inference strategies in reading comprehension. *Cognition and Instruction*, 5(3), 193–222.

Rizzolatti, G. & Craighero, L. (2004). The mirror neuron system. *Annu. Rev. Neurosci.*, 27, 169–192.

Rizzolatti, G., Fadiga, L., Fogassi, L. & Gallese, V. (1996). Premotor cortex and the recognition of motor actions. *Cogn. Brain Res.* 3, 131–41.

Rorty, R. (1989). *Contingency, irony and solidarity*. New York: Cambridge University Press.

Rosenblatt, L. (1965/1995). *Literature as exploration*. New York: MLA.

Williams, R. (1958). *Culture and society, 1780–1950*. New York: Columbia UP.

Simon, H.A. (1994). Literary criticism: A cognitive approach. *Stanford Humanities Review*, Suppl. 4:1, 1–26.

Zunshine, L. (2006). *Why we read fiction: Theory of mind and the novel*. Columbus: The Ohio State University Press.

4

LITERATURE AND CRITICAL THINKING

How Fiction Makes Us Think

> If you want nonstop high-level sociocognitive complexity, simultaneous with nonstop active reorganization of perceptions and inferences, only fiction delivers. Teach less of it, and only students whose parents encourage them to read a lot of fiction on their own will still do well. The less fortunate others will end up with poor vocabularies and grades.
>
> *(Zunshine, L., 2013, p. 5)*

The argument that literature is primarily taught because it inspires deep, or critical, thinking among its readers is possibly the most commonly stated reason for including literary reading in the secondary school curriculum. The justification that reading fiction helps a young person think better seems palatable to those in a variety of disciplines who value discoverable facts rather than the much harder-to-define aesthetic appreciation or subjective education for personal growth. The critical thinking argument for teaching literature is a safer one to make than the identification or empathy argument—more scholarly, less personal, and more rigorous, at least as rigor is currently defined by many policy-makers, pundits, and school administrators. And English teachers have, by and large, accepted this critical thinking argument as well, planning lessons and curricula that propose to teach literature to enhance the critical or "deep" thinking of their students. The critical thinking argument is also often used when defending the humanities as an academic discipline in general: we read books not for the experience of reading itself, or for the content of the text, or for how reading can change our self understanding, but for the discrete "skills" that reading can teach us and that can subsequently be applied to other more vocational, quantifiable endeavors—skills such as critical thinking.

I am certainly not opposed to the teaching of critical thinking, provided that teaching decontextualized thinking is something that can even be done. However, it can seem a reductionist answer to the "why teach literature?" argument, an easy response with which few will argue. Do we use the critical thinking argument to forestall a real conversation about the importance of literary reading, an argument many of us don't know how to make convincingly any other way? I know when I have used that argument in the past to defend literary teaching and reading, I have always felt as if I was somehow being insincere—or at least incomplete.

When I teach pre-service English teachers they never question the importance of critical thinking as central to the ELA (English Language Arts) curriculum, although there is often a sense of confusion about what it is exactly and how they will know when their future students do it. They have heard the phrase many times, and they know it's important (who's going to doubt the need for think-ing?), but initially it's simply an abstract concept to them, without ties to concrete classroom strategies or real student responses. Once pre-service teachers have a sense of what critical thinking looks like in a classroom (i.e., making connections among texts, asking questions, making comparisons and inferences) they can start imagining how reading literature might be consistent with a "teaching for critical thinking" approach. Hopefully, they will also see how when we discuss thinking about literary texts, the processes at work are actually more varied and complex that many textbooks and curricular materials suggest, particularly when critical thinking is the only justification provided for literary study.

The idea of teaching literature for critical thinking grows from literacy research, research that advocates the teaching of reading to deepen and enrich student thinking. Such thinking skills are seen as essential to prepare students for success on standardized tests as well as in future classes and vocations. A notable scholar in this area is Judith Langer (1990; 1992; 1994; 1995), who has spent a great deal of her career researching and thinking about literature, literacy, and thinking. Even though she has written many scholarly works exploring thinking about literature, in many of them she is concerned about using literature for the teaching of generic critical thinking (1995). She is worried about focusing on discrete, transferable skills as reasons for teaching literature, at the expense of more holistic understandings of reader response and what reading can offer readers. She recently writes:

> Since the early 21st century ... there has been a turning away from the centrality of literature in the English and English language arts curriculum as a source of intellectual, moral, civic and/or ethical development, and a focus on English and ELA coursework as preparation for a set of more general literacy skills considered necessary to do well in college and the job world.
>
> *(Langer, 2014, p. 162)*

Hence, the Common Core State Standards for college and career readiness. Discrete literacy skills, including such things as making predictions, making inferences, or connecting and comparing texts, are obviously valued in the very name of the Common Core State Standards themselves, which are subtitled "preparing America's students for college and career" (www.corestandards.org). Purposes for teaching and reading literature have to be pretty narrowly, and concretely, defined if the purpose is solely to prepare a young reader for the next academic class or a particular set of job skills. Many of the aspects of literary reading mentioned in the previous chapters of this book, including identification and empathy, would be irrelevant in such a pragmatic approach. In fact, two of the four anchor standards for reading in grades K–12 ("key ideas and details" and "craft and structure") could arguably largely be met through the study of abridged or annotated texts of either fiction or nonfiction, as they focus on analyzing decontextualized features, such as word meaning, sentence/paragraph structure, and the summary of key points or details (see National Governors Association, 2012a, 2012b). Why spend time reading a complete novel at all?

Langer is concerned that this increased emphasis on "skills and strategies" (p. 162) will result in fewer, complete literary texts being taught (and read) at the secondary level, with nonfiction and content area selections being favored instead. However, Langer argues that fictional narrative literature teaches cognitive skills that other texts cannot match (p. 162). So while she is not in favor of literature being taught simply to facilitate generic critical thinking in the service of other disciplines, she does admit, and I agree, that the literary experience *can* result in analytical, creative, and imaginative thinking that other reading experiences do not. The process is just more complex than skills-oriented approaches can explain.

A concept related to the teaching of literature is the teaching of reading, which, particularly in middle schools, has often replaced the teaching of literature. The teaching of reading tends of focus on reading "strategies" that can be applied to any type of text to improve comprehension and, by association, critical thinking. Many literacy researchers have focused on the teaching of reading, not the teaching of literature, even if they see literature as occupying an important place in the English classroom (see Beers & Probst, 2012; Tovani, 2000; Appleman, 2010). Reading strategies usually are defined as specific, observable behaviors that teachers can teach to improve their students' comprehension of and thinking about a text, including activities such as note-taking, making personal connections, journaling, asking questions, predicting and visualizing (Tovani, 2000).

While such strategies are described as being in the service of more complex and holistic responses to texts, there is doubt that they always, or even often, lead to such deeper cognitive and affective response (Rosenshine and Meister, 1994). Perhaps the students only learn the strategy—for example, how to journal or ask questions or predict what's going to happen next—but they don't become more proficient readers of a complete text; maybe they don't experience anything more substantive in their literary reading, emotional or cognitive response, or narrative engagement after learning the strategy. Perhaps the teaching of strategies even takes time way from other more important or complex literary experiences

(Sinatra et al., 2002). The most recent comprehension research has moved away from strategy instruction and begun to focus on open-ended classroom discussion as a way to promote reading comprehension (McKeown et al., 2009; Nystrand, 2006). These researchers see discussion about texts as a way for young readers to understand how grappling with competing perspectives and points of view can lead to deeper understandings.

Most college literature courses attempt to use dialogue about texts as a way to understand them. However, in addition to the dialogic component, critical thinking about literature at the post-secondary level often involves close reading, explication, parsing text, or concentrated attention to a text at hand. Close reading is finding the meaning of a text, which is often seen as singular or identifiable, through closely looking at the individual words, phrases, and clauses and the ways in which they unfold. Traditionally, when doing a close reading, there is little attention paid to sociocultural context, reader response, or authorial intent or identity.

New Critical theorist I.A. Richards is commonly associated with the notion of close reading and seeking meaning that can be found within a text (see *Practical Criticism: A Study of Literary Judgment*, 1956). The notion of close reading has morphed over the last twenty-five years from a relatively context-devoid approach into more post-modernist and sociocultural readings of texts, often informed by schools of thought such as feminism, new historicism, Marxism, disability studies, critical race theory, and postcolonial studies. In these approaches close reading of the words on the page still happens and is valued as a way to think about and understand texts; however, more than the new critics ever imagined, these approaches aim to speak to and reveal the experiences of diverse people as depicted in literature, and even promote social change.

So where do we go next with this idea of reading for critical thinking, both at the secondary and post-secondary levels? Michael Roth in *The Chronicle of Higher Education* (2010) argues for a "transition from critical thinking to practical exploration" (p. 6), where students of the humanities will be more inclined to make new meaning through collaborations and interdisciplinary connections, not simply deconstruct how the arguments of others are shortsighted or wrong. He hopes that critical thinking will be enriched with "the capacity for empathy and comprehension that stretches the self," rather than reinforce the contemporary tendency toward criticism that rejects alternative, unfamiliar or contradictory ideas (p. 3).

Such an argument is similar to that of philosopher and humanist Martha Nussbaum, who argues for the close association between cognition and emotion, or the critical and the affective faculties. In fact, she writes that emotions are intimately connected to cognition, that they are "intelligent responses to the perception of value" (2001, p. 1) or "part and parcel of ethical reasoning" (p. 1). If she is correct, then it should be impossible to talk about critical thinking as reader response apart from the other responses explored in this book, responses that are clearly more emotional, affective, and subjective.

What is Critical Thinking?

Critical thinking became popular among educators in the 1940s, when Edward M. Glaser (1941) reported on an experiment which concluded that critical thinking has three components: 1) open, reflective attitude; 2) knowledge of logical inquiry; and 3) skill in applying such inquiry. In 1962, Robert H. Ennis published "A Concept of Critical Thinking" in the *Harvard Educational Review*, which moved the study of critical thinking into the arena of teacher education, exploring how teachers could best facilitate critical thinking or critical analysis among their students. Since that time, critical thinking has been a common theme in colleges of education and in-service teacher workshops, as well as in textbooks and teaching guides. Critical thinking is defined as follows by the Foundation for Critical Thinking:

> Critical thinking is the intellectually disciplined process of actively and skill-fully conceptualizing, applying, analyzing, synthesizing, and/or evaluating information gathered from, or generated by, observation, experience, reflection, reasoning, or communication, as a guide to belief and action. In its exemplary form, it is based on universal intellectual values that transcend subject matter divisions: clarity, accuracy, precision, consistency, relevance, sound evidence, good reasons, depth, breadth, and fairness.
>
> *(www.criticalthinking.org/pages/defining-critical-thinking/766)*

The definition, by its own admission, is transferable across subject matters and areas of study; critical thinking is a generalized process that can be taught and/or learned and then applied widely throughout life.

While it can be argued that critical thinking skills have been taught for a very long time, perhaps beginning with Socratic questioning over two thousand years ago, since the 1940s critical thinking and teaching critical thinking "skills" have become somewhat of an educational industry in the US, as researchers and educational publishers have disseminated much information about critical thinking for teacher consumption (see www.criticalthinking.org/pages/high-school-teachers/807 for some examples). English teachers have likewise been inundated with critical thinking guides and curricular approaches to teaching language and literature that emphasize critical thinking. They have been encouraged to use literature as one way to teach this supposedly generalizable, essential and definable skill.

Below is a visual image of how I see the relationship between critical thinking and the teaching and reading of literature, as it seems to be primarily under-stood by contemporary educators, researchers and scholars. The addition of context isn't always recognized in more simplified versions of critical thinking in response to literature, but when it is considered, a more complex, holistic cognitive response occurs.

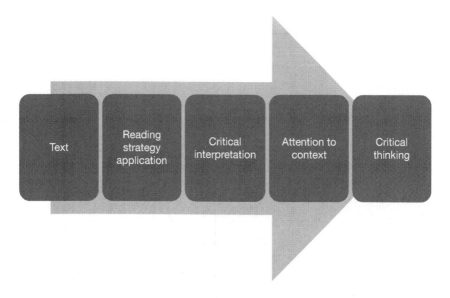

FIGURE 4.1 Literary response as critical thinking. As a reader decodes a text and makes meaning of it, attention to context can lead to complex critical response.

Researching Relationships Between Critical Thinking and Literature

While much of the research I have found about the benefits of teaching literature to adolescents has focused on more holistic understandings of reader response to texts, a few have focused solely or primarily on cognitive, or thinking, skills. Surprisingly, there has been little empirical research demonstrating a clear connection between reading literature and the development of critical thought. In fact, in Hakemulder's (2000) exhaustive overview of research studies exploring how reading may change readers, he found only one reliable study (Bird, 1984) linking reading literature to critical thinking. Much of the scholarship that does exist can be categorized under the broader epistemological umbrella of the reading comprehension of elementary aged students, including related thinking skills such as making inferences and evaluating authors' messages. While critical thinking and comprehension might not always be defined in the same way, reading researchers seem more likely to address the issue of comprehension, as it is more narrow and easily definable, and, therefore, perhaps more compatible with empirical research methods, than the more nebulous, context driven, critical thinking. What follows is a brief review of research on reading comprehension that has implications for critical thinking through literary study.

To begin, research on reading comprehension has shown that time spent reading increases the ability to comprehend. According to a synthesis of research conducted by Fielding and Pearson (1994) research studies in the 70s and 80s revealed that prior knowledge was closely related to comprehension, and a reader could gain knowledge through reading (Beck et al. 1982; Hansen and Pearson, 1983). Additionally, a statistical relationship has been found between how much time students spend reading and how well they comprehend what they read (Anderson et al., 1988). Since students who are at lower reading levels will often be asked by teachers to spend more time on worksheets and drills rather than reading, research has shown that the additional reading time given to stronger readers actually widens the gap between good and poor readers; so, in other words, the skill and drill does not help (Allington, 1983; Stanovich, 1986). Such research is support for including reading in a curriculum not only as homework, but as classroom practice. An important related note is that while there has been no direct connection found in research between reading choice and improved comprehension, there have been demonstrated connections between student choice of reading material and motivation to read, which is related to learning in several studies (Anderson et al., 1987; Worthy and McKool, 1996; Guthrie and Wigfield, 2000).

Another area of research in the '80s and '90s focused on the extent to which the teaching of reading strategies improved reading comprehension. Such explicitly taught, task-oriented strategies are somewhat controversial, as I discussed earlier in this chapter, as they tend to reduce the act of reading to discreet, decontextualized behaviors. However, some research studies have shown that teaching specific comprehension strategies, such as using background knowledge, understanding story structure through understanding narrative conventions, and identifying main ideas, can improve reading skills of students (Hansen and Pearson, 1983; Baumann, 1984; Fitzgerald and Spiegel, 1983). Research also demonstrated that teacher modeling of these strategies was important (Duffy et al. 1988, Paris et al. 1991), as was student guided practice with using these strategies (Pearson and Dole, 1987).

To move students from simply accepting the interpretations of texts as pro- vided by a teacher to forming their own, some researchers and theorists have advocated literary discussions that allow for the sharing of student personal respon- ses and interpretations, in addition to answering teacher questions, a practice followed by many ELA teachers. This research has shown that when engaging in open literary discussions, students often offer a range of responses from literal to critical and use others' opinions to refine their own understandings of a text (Eeds & Wells, 1989; Raphael et al., 1992; Rogers, 1991). In other words, these open discussions, replete with a variety of expressed opinions and responses, tend to lead to deeper, critical readings, even if they do seem a little unorganized.

Last, Linda M. Phillips in a 1988 research study found that high proficiency 6th grade readers most frequently used the reading strategies of shifting focus when an impasse is reached, confirming prior expectations while reading, and empathi- zing with story content (p. 193). In these ways, the young readers successfully made inferences about texts, which she defines as a "constructive thinking process because the reader expands knowledge by proposing and evaluating competing hypotheses about the meaning of a text," (p. 194), a definition that sounds similar to definitions of critical thinking. In Phillips' study the most skilled young readers tended to use empathy building as a reading strategy that allowed them to make inferences about, and therefore understand, narrative texts. Phillips argues that for her young participants empathy was a strategy they consciously chose and applied to their reading, not one that may have come naturally and subconsciously, as it might for adult readers (p. 208). Phillips' study might be an argument for teaching empathy building strategies as part of the reading process for young readers, explicitly modeling for them how to empathize with narrative characters and events as a pathway to deeper understandings of the story.

The Pedagogy of Critical Thinking

Problem-based learning

Problem-based learning is not a pedagogy that is often talked about in relationship to literature or literature teaching. Alternately, it began as an approach used by medical schools to help small groups of students "problem solve" about patient cases by applying their classroom knowledge to a real-world setting. Since that time, problem-based learning has expanded and become popular in other disciplines, such as science, engineering, mathematics, business and law. While English and literature have not normally followed this model of instruction, problem-based learning seems consistent with Beach, Thein, and Webb's (2012) notion of a "literacy practices approach" (p. 42) to literature instruction, and which attempts to structure literacy activities within real-world, relevant projects to complete or problems to solve. Even if a teacher does not purposefully undertake a literacy practices approach, problem-based instruction may be applicable to a pedagogy of teaching literature to encourage critical thinking, particularly if the teacher believes that teaching isolated thinking "skills" is not sufficient and he or she wishes students to think critically within the context of a larger issue, concept, question or idea. Following the pattern from earlier chapters, I first define the concept below, then I connect the central idea of this chapter (in this case, critical thinking and literature) to the selected pedagogical approach. Finally, I return to the visual model presented earlier in this chapter to frame my final thoughts about the pedagogy and what it might accomplish.

What is problem-based learning?

Problem-based learning is pretty much what it says it is: learning concepts and skills, or exploring ideas or notions, within the context of a structured *problem,* a problem often, but not always, presented by the teacher for the students to consider. When "doing" problem-based learning in a classroom, students work in small groups to identify what they already know and what they will need to know to solve a problem or understand an issue or concept. They also must figure out how to access or find the information or knowledge that will help them solve the given problem. The teacher acts as guide or facilitator, directing, nudging and motivating the small groups of learners. Problem-based learning bears similarities to "experiential learning," a concept closely linked to educator and philosopher John Dewey (1938/1997). The difference is that problem-based learning primarily takes place in a classroom, not in a real-world setting, even though relevant or authentic problems may be presented for students to consider.

While this model might imitate much of what goes on in adult workplaces, at least the more creative ones, it also has potential for learning in various content areas in school. If students collaborate intellectually and socially to explore an issue or idea (or perhaps the theme or significance of a work of fiction), they will surely encounter diverse ideas and opinions that will require discussion, cooperation, and negotiation. While problem-based learning may not seem like much more than group work or group discussion, I counter that if it is based on a central, driving question (or "problem") that guides the group's talk, research, writing, creation or experimentation, then it becomes a more focused and poten-tially more intellectually demanding exercise. Some believe that problem-based learning is too difficult to implement, too hard for students who are not used to such autonomy, or just too unstructured and unorganized. Proponents disagree, as they argue that problem-based learning can enhance critical thinking, collab-oration, and communication skills, as students work through a problem or issue (see Barrett, 2010; Sendag and Odabasi, 2009 for arguments in favor). I think problem-based learning has similar potential in secondary school literature classes, as students connect fiction to problems in their communities and cultures and examine how the literature can both speak to these issues and prompt further research, discussion, imaginative creation, or writing as the problem is explored and interrogated.

Connections between problem-based learning and the experience of critical thinking

Problem-based learning theories often mention critical thinking as one of the goals and outcomes; students solving problems must engage in many cognitive processes that are usually called critical thought, such as comparing and contra-sting, prioritizing information, connecting various texts, predicting, inferring, and relating content to self. As I describe above, these processes are also often valued when teachers teach literature, and such cognitive processes are almost always encouraged (or required) of students during class discussions, essay writing, or exams. However, the problem-based approach has the potential of avoiding a major pitfall I mention earlier in this chapter, the problem of teaching decontex-tualized "thinking skills" or thinking strategies outside of a real reason to engage in them. If students are working with a literary text, and perhaps seeing it as a pathway into solving or re-considering a problem, then there is a reason to infer, or predict, or compare/contrast. And, as I also mentioned earlier, this cognition will not, cannot, happen with the affective response also occurring— the identification, the empathizing, or even the compulsion to act.

As in the previous chapters, I end by returning to the visual model for critical thinking I created and included earlier in this chapter. As you can see by revisiting it, a reader ideally reads a text, comprehends it, begins to understand it, and finally connects it to larger meanings, ideas, issues, personal experience and/or other texts. Then complex critical thinking can result. It seems like problem-based learning suits this model.

BOX 4.1   SAMPLE LITERATURE LESSON TO ENCOURAGE CRITICAL THINKING

Contributed by Shaylyn Marks, formerly of Westfield Middle School, Westfield, Indiana.

Pre-reading activity: create a utopian community in response to Lois Lowry's *The Giver*

While reading *The Giver*, you will be challenged to analyze the futuristic society that Lois Lowry creates for readers. The reading of this novel should test your thinking about how we live together in our current society and whether the society Lowry created for the characters in the novel is a utopia or a dystopia (or both). This conclusion will depend on your point of view and perspective.

So what is a utopia? What are desirable, and feasible, characteristics of one? For this activity, you will be asked to work in small groups to create your own utopian society. First, you will analyze our current society to figure out how you would make your constructed society "better." Here are some things to think about:

- What would have to be added to our own society to make it perfect?
- What would be lost in this quest for perfection?

Second, take your thoughts about the above questions and apply them to your improved, created community. Below are some things to include when describing this improved community:

- Community name
- System of government

- Physical description
- How people spend their days
- How the community can change or grow
- Roles played by history or memory
- Anything else relevant to *your* community

Third, you will present your community to the rest of the class.

As we read *The Giver*, you will hone your ideas about a utopian society and continue to consider the strengths and weaknesses of your created community.

References

Anderson, R.C., Shirey, L., Wilson, P.T. & Fielding, L.G. (1987). Interestingness of children's reading material. In Snow, R. & Farr, M. (Eds), *Aptitude, learning and instruction. Vol. 3: Cognitive and affective process analyses*. Mahwah, N.J.: Erlbaum.

Anderson, R.C., Wilson, P.T. & Fielding, L.G. (1988). Growth in reading and how children spend their time outside of school. *Reading Research Quarterly*, 23, 285–303.

Allington, R.L. (1983). The reading instruction provided readers of different reading abilities. *Elementary School Journal*, 83, 548–559.

Appleman, D. (2010). *Adolescent literacy and the teaching of reading: Lessons for teachers of literature*. Urbana, IL: NCTE.

Barrett, T. (2010). The problem-based learning process as finding and being in flow. *Innovations in Education and Teaching International*, 47(2), unpaged, published online.

Baumann, J.F. (1984). Effectiveness of a direct instruction paradigm for teaching main idea comprehension. *Reading Research Quarterly*, 20, 93–108.

Beach, R., Thein, A.H. & Webb, A. (2012). *Teaching to exceed the English language arts common core state standards: A literacy practices approach for 6–12 classrooms*. New York: Routledge.

Beck, I.L., Omanson, R.C. & McDeown, M.G. (1982). An instructional redesign of reading lessons: Effects on comprehension. *Reading Research Quarterly*, 17, 462–481.

Beers, K. & Probst, R.E. (2012). *Notice and note: Strategies for close reading*. Portsmouth, NH: Heinemann.

Bird, J.J. (1984). *Effects of fifth graders' attitudes and critical thinking/reading skills resulting from a junior great books program*. PhD Diss. New Brunswick: Rutgers University Press.

Dewey, J. (1938/1997). *Experience and education*, reprint edition. New York: Free Press.

Duffy, G., Roehler, L. & Hermann, B. (1988). Modeling mental processes helps poor readers become strategic readers. *The Reading Teacher*, 41, 762–767.

Eeds, M. & Wells, D. (1989). Grand conversations: An exploration of meaning construction in literature study groups. *Research in the Teaching of English*, 23, 4–29.

Ennis, R.H. (1962). A concept of critical thinking. *Harvard Educational Review*, 32(1), 81–111.

Fielding, L.G. & Pearson, P.D. (1994). Synthesis of research/reading comprehension: What works. *Teaching for Understanding*, 51(5), 62–68.

Fitzgerald, J. & Spiegel, D.L. (1983). Enhancing children's reading comprehension through instruction in narrative structure. *Journal of Reading Behavior*, 15(2), 1–17.

Foundation for Critical Thinking. The Critical Thinking community – High school teachers. Retrieved April 22, 2014 from www.criticalthinking.org/pages/high-school-teachers/807

Glaser, E.M. (1941). *An experiment in the development of critical thinking.* New York: Bureau of Publications, Teachers College, Columbia University.

Guthrie, J.T. & Wigfield, A. (2000). Engagement and motivation in reading. In M.L. Kamil and P.B. Mosenthal (Eds), *Handbook of reading research*, Vol. III, pp. 403–422. Mahwah, N.J.: Lawrence Erlbaum.

Hakemulder, J. (2000). *The moral laboratory: Experiments examining the effects of reading literature on social perception and moral self-concept.* Amsterdam/Philadelphia: John Benjamins.

Hansen, J. and Pearson, P.D. (1983). An instructional study: Improving inferential comprehension of good and poor fourth-grade readers. *Journal of Educational Psychology*, 75, 821–829.

Langer, J.A. (1990). The process of understanding: Reading for literary and informational purposes. *Research in the Teaching of English*, 24(3), 229–260.

Langer, J.A. (1992). Discussion as exploration: Literature and the horizon of possibilities. In G. Newell & R. Durst (Eds), *The role of discussion and writing in the teaching and learning of literature*, pp. 23–24. Norwood, MA: Christopher Gordon Publishers.

Langer, J.A. (1994). Focus on research: A response-based approach to reading literature. *Language Arts*, 71, 203–211.

Langer, J.A. (1995). Literature and learning to think. *Journal of Curriculum and Supervision*, 10(3), 207–226.

Langer, J. (2014). The role of literature and literary reasoning in English language arts and English classrooms. In K.S. Goodman, R.C. Calfee, & Y.M. Goodman (Eds), *Whose knowledge counts in government literacy policies? Why expertise matters*, pp. 161–167. New York: Routledge.

McKeown, M.G., Beck, I.L. & Blake, R.G.K. (2009). Rethinking reading comprehension instruction: A comparison of instruction for strategies and content approaches. *Reading Research Quarterly*, 44(3), 218–253.

National Governors Association Center for Best Practices & Council of Chief State School Officers. (2012a). *Common Core State Standards.* Washington, DC: Authors. Retrieved from www.corestandards.org

National Governors Association Center for Best Practices & Council of Chief State School Officers. (2012b). *English Language Arts Standards-Anchor Standards-College and Career Readiness Anchor Standards for Reading.* Washington, DC: Authors. Retrieved from www.corestandards.org/ELA-Literacy/CCRA/R/

Nussbaum, M. (2001). *Upheavals of thought: The Intelligence of emotions.* New York: Cambridge University Press.

Nystrand, M. (2006). Research on the role of classroom discourse as it affects reading comprehension. *Research in the Teaching of English*, 40(4), 392–412.

Paris, S.G., Wasik, B.A. & Turner, J.C. (1991). The development of strategic readers. In R. Barr, M. Kamil, P. Mosenthal & P.D. Pearson (Eds), *Handbook of Reading Research: Vol. II.* New York: Longman.

Pearson, P.D. & Dole, J.A. (1987). Explicit comprehension instruction: A review of research and a new conceptualization of instruction. *Elementary School Journal*, 88(2), 151–165.

Phillips, L.M. (1988). Young readers' inference strategies in reading comprehension. *Cognition and Instruction*, 5(3), 193–222.

Raphael, T., McMahon, S., Goatley, V., Bentley, J., Boyd, F., Pardo, L. & Woodman, D. (1992). Research directions: Literature and discussion in the reading program. *Language Arts*, 69, 54–61.

Richards, I.A. (1956). *Practical criticism: A study of literary judgment.* New York: Mariner Books.

Rogers, T. (1991). Students as literary critics: The interpretive experiences, beliefs, and processes of ninth-grade students. *Journal of Reading Behavior*, 23, 391–423.

Rosenshine, B. & Meister, C. (1994). Reciprocal teaching: A review of the research. *Review of Educational Research*, 64(4), 479–530.

Roth, M.S. (2010). Beyond critical thinking. *The Chronicle of Higher Education.* Retrieved April 15, 2014 from https://chronicle.com/article/Beyond-Critical-Thinking/63288/

Scriven, M. & Paul, R. (1987). Defining critical thinking. Retrieved from www.criticalthinking.org/pages/defining-critical-thinking/766

Sendag, S. & Odabasi, F.H. (2009). Effects of an online problem based learning course on content knowledge acquisition and critical thinking skills. *Computers & Education*, 53, 132–141.

Sinatra, G.M., Brown, K.J. & Reynolds, R.E. (2002). Implications of cognitive resource allocation for comprehension strategies instruction. In C.C. Block & M. Pressley (Eds), *Comprehension instruction: Research-based best practices*, pp. 62–76. New York: Guilford Press.

Stanovich, K. (1986). Matthew effects in reading: Some consequences of individual differences in the acquisition of literacy. *Reading Research Quarterly*, 21, 360–407.

Tovani, C. (2000). *I read it, but I don't get it: Comprehension strategies for adolescent readers.* Portland, ME: Stenhouse.

Worthy, J. & McKool, S.S. (1996). Students who say they hate to read: The importance of opportunity, choice, and access. *The National Reading Conference Yearbook.*

Zunshine, L. (2013). Why fiction does it better. *The Chronicle of Higher Education.* Retrieved on December 10, 2013, from www.lisazunshine.net/index%20page%20files/Why%20Fiction%20Does%20It%20Better.pdf

5

LITERATURE AND SOCIAL ACTION

Can Reading Change What We Do?

A self without a story contracts into the thinness of its personal pronoun.

(Crites, S., 1986, p. 172)

I asked my students in a recent graduate class in young adult literature if they could remember ever changing their actions because of a novel or story they read, particularly when they were adolescents. A few students raised their hands and said yes. After reading Stephenie Meyer's *Twilight*, they might have worn a "Team Edward" or "Team Jacob" T-shirt, or after reading Meg Cabot's *The Princess Diaries* they began keeping a journal. However, there weren't actually too many examples offered, and the ones that were offered were fairly superficial. When I tried to think of my own reading life, it was likewise hard for me to come up with specific, concrete examples of behavior change that I could link to a book; however, at the same time, I was just sure that reading had changed me, had changed my life and how I acted in some important way. Concrete evidence was just hard to find.

This chapter has been in many ways the most difficult to write. But it may also be the most important, as it really is *the* issue that the rest of the chapters lead up to, the real reason for being interested in all of the other arguments for teaching literature in the secondary school. I have discussed in the earlier chapters how clear links do indeed exist, described both in theoretical and empirical terms, among reading literature, identifying with characters, increased feelings of empathy for others, and thinking more deeply. However, this chapter tackles the twenty-thousand-dollar question for teachers of literature: can reading and responding to literature change behavior? Can reading literature, with all its various and sundry effects on feeling and thinking, also result in *doing* something differently? Treating others better? Making improved decisions about how to act in the world?

These questions are complex and hard to answer. And even if they could be answered in the affirmative, that, yes, reading literature definitely changes the behavior of readers, such confidence in the power of reading could be a double-edged sword. Understanding reading as behavior-changing could also be used in the service of censorship. If something is that powerful, maybe we should be afraid of it. Cautious of doing it. Avoid it, even. But, alternately, if reading only changes how you *think* about things, and not how you make decisions in the three-dimensional world, is it really as powerful as literature teachers and scholars may think? Does thinking (and/or feeling) always change acting? Self-reporting on a survey that you empathize, or identify, with a character is one thing: actually translating these reported feelings to real world actions is quite another.

A different, but perhaps related, question is whether narratives can change *who* we are, in addition to *what* we do. This "who" question is addressed in the previous chapters, but primarily in terms of how we respond to others; e.g., narrative experience can change how a reader thinks or feels about other people. This chapter instead focuses inward on the self, the reader him or herself. Does reading change the reader's identity? I'll start with the easier question to answer: can reading literature change who we are, and then move to the more difficult one, can reading literature change what we do.

Many philosophers and theorists throughout the decades, including Campbell (1972), Bruner (1986), and Polkinghorne (1991), have discussed how stories can affect identity. In the 1960s and 1970s, the field of narratology was concerned primarily with literary study and analyzing the role of narratives in texts (Frye, 1964; Booth, 1961); more recently, interest in narrative has expanded to include sociocultural examinations of the role of narrative in identity construction, culture, and communicative contexts (Jahn, 1999). Many theorists, such as Bruner, claim that narratives not only *structure* human experience after the fact, but they also *change* it; the very act of story-telling not only depicts our experience, it changes how we remember and understand it. The advice goes, if you want to change your sense of self, change how you tell your story (Wortham, 2001). Furthermore, if narratives have the power to change how we see or think about ourselves, they could potentially change how we act. For example, if our narratives of self include stories of ourselves as altruistic, maybe we will be altruistic; if our stories depict us as selfish, perhaps we will act selfishly. So to extend the argument, if personal, internalized stories about experience can affect identity, could fictional narratives likewise be used by the reader to construct and re-construct self? If so, how and when does this happen with literary reading?

Richard Gerrig (1993) does not believe that reading literature regularly leads to behavior change. Similar to Norman Holland (2009), he tends to think that readers (or viewers) of fictional stories will most often "stop" or inhibit behaviors in response to a story when that behavior is clearly not "functional" (Gerrig, 1993, p. 189). However, even though he believes this to be the case most of the time, Gerrig does remind us of exceptions, of times when fiction has changed behavior. Examples include viewers of the movie *Jaws* who stopped swimming after seeing the film, and readers of Sherlock Holmes novels who believe that since many aspects of Doyle's London were accurate, perhaps Holmes was a real person whom they can locate there (Gerrig, 1993, pp. 207–208). So sometimes fiction *does* change real-life behavior, particularly when it tweaks powerful memories or emotions, even if the pre-frontal cortex inhibits most non-helpful behaviors in response to fiction.

If fictional experience does influence behavior, then Plato's fears of the poets might be justified; perhaps authors of imaginative texts seeking to imitate and comment upon life do inspire dangerous emotions and behavior which might otherwise be repressed. Many censors feel the same way about so-called "dangerous" literature—if readers, particularly young, inexperienced ones, read about a risky behavior such as drinking or having sex, won't they be more likely to imitate that behavior? However, as I discussed in the chapters on identification and empathy, the reading process, even of young readers, is likely much more complex than the imitation argument implies, making these fears seemingly unfounded. However, such suspicion persists, and if literature teachers argue that books change people for the better, how can we squelch the opposite argument, that books might change people for the worse?

Assuming that we accept the argument that literature might, just might, change behavior, how exactly does this process occur? And what kind of literature changes a reader the most successfully and the most positively? Based on the previously summarized research, the process seems to be that readers, 1) identify with fictional characters, settings, or events; 2) empathize with said characters; and 3) are moved to related action. Additionally, in the literature already cited, there is evidence that so-called literary texts, the type with "foregrounded" literary elements, figures, and tropes, result in identification and empathy most frequently. However, it is also clear that the skill, experience and expertise of the reader also matters—as does the type of classroom, or otherwise dialogic, experience a reader has with a text. Those who were encouraged through classroom discussions to empathize or identify, for example, seem more prone to do so, and do so in more complex ways.

It seems important in this chapter to spend a few moments discussing young adult literature as a special case. Young adult literature, as differentiated from adult literature, seems to have an explicitly pedagogical function: many authors will say they write their works to influence young people, and many Young Adult (YA) books are literally taught in classrooms or offered in school libraries. Many YA books seem to be striving first and foremost for teen identification with characters and settings, as they attempt to create real-life worlds similar to those actual teens experience. In this way, these authors hope to use bibliotherapy to help teenagers handle problems, make decisions, and learn lessons. However, does social realism work to influence behavior in this way? Does it really teach the kind of lessons the authors hope? I argued in the introduction to my edited collection *Young Adult Literature and Adolescent Identity Across Cultures and Classrooms* (Alsup, 2010) that:

it is important to work with students to recognize both the similarities and the differences between the text and their own experiences. The recognition of these differences, or the so-called "gap" between the reader's real life and the world created in the text, is essential ... [W]ithout this gap, and without study of the gap, it is difficult to create the so-called education imagination or holistic reader—the reader who is able both to *experience* a textual world and to *view* it with distanced aesthetic awareness.

(p. 11)

As I discussed in Chapter 2, true identification is a more complex experience than seeing a one-to-one correspondence between oneself and a character in a novel. Therefore, even if some YA authors are attempting to instruct through their books, and even if teachers actually do teach the books in the classroom, true reader engagement with the text means much more than simple recognition and knee jerk imitation.

What is Social Action?

What is meant by the phrase "social action"? Primarily, I am referring to behaviors engaged in by individuals that affect others around them and, by association, the context in which they all live. Related, but slightly different, are the concepts of prosocial behavior, helping behavior, and altruism, which assume that the actor is doing something that he or she knows will not directly benefit him or herself, but will benefit another individual, sometimes to the detriment of the actor. Many of the research studies I summarize below will use all of these terms interchangeably, while others will differentiate among them.

Max Weber, a German sociologist and philosopher in the late 19th and early 20th centuries, perhaps first discussed the concept of social action. He believed that social action happened through subjective interactions among individuals who make decisions to act based on their emotional, habitual, or goal-oriented states of mind (Runciman, 1978, p. 28). In Weber's theory, social action can lead to positive social change in a particular context. In this way, Weber found individuals to have great power in society to improve their lives. In his 1922 *The Nature of Social Action,* he defined social action as, "the human behavior when and to the extent that the agent or agents see it as *subjectively meaningful*" (Runciman, p. 7). Such a view of social action that empowers human beings to change their situations is in contrast to other sociological theories, which see humans as more constrained by economic forces (e.g., Marxism) or by bias and injustice (e.g., Feminism).

While some may see social action theory as too optimistic and idealistic, Weber saw the power of human decision-making and intentional action, even in the face of bureaucratic structures and unfair social hierarchies. Such confidence in the power of individuals working together to create positive change is relevant to our study of literature as possibly transformative. If there is any hope that reading and responding to narrative fiction might result in positive behavior change, altruism, or helping behavior, there must be some truth to the theory that individuals *can* decide to behave in certain ways and hence change their social contexts, cultures, or communities. If one does not believe in the power of individuals to effect social change, even in the face of great opposition, there is little reason to hope that literary reading can be instrumental, or even beneficial, to this process. Additionally, as Weber's notion of social action was inherently rooted in subjectivity, literary response, also deeply subjective, seems a theoretically consistent motivation for such actions.

Closely connected to social action is the concept of social justice, which is a much-discussed concept in English education scholarship (see Adams, et al., 2010; Apple, 2006; Ayers, 1998; Bender-Slack, 2010; Cochran-Smith, 1999 and 2004; Miller et al., 2008; Nieto and Bode, 2011). Usually, social justice is discussed by English teacher educators who are seeking ways to help pre-service teachers think about educating youth with a social justice approach or sensibility, promoting fairness, equity, and respect for all students no matter their race, gender, sexual orientation, gender identity, or disability status. Social justice approaches to teaching tend to emphasize behaviors or actions that support such ideologies. Perhaps not surprisingly, many ELA teachers and teacher educators see literary reading and response as one way to encourage awareness and understanding of many different types of people, cultures, and communities among their students. The hope is that through such narrative experiences, empathy will result, which may lead to attitudinal changes toward individuals different from the readers themselves. In fact, as I described in Chapter 3, there is indeed some research that bears out these hypothesized connections between reading, empathy, and positive attitude change. So while direct connections between reading and behavior change are still hard to prove, such desired social action often seems ideologically connected to a wider aspiration for social justice.

Below is an image of how I understand narrative fiction reading can connect to social action, as can be ascertained through a synthesis of the research about reading, empathy and identification, as well as the small body of research directly linking narrative experience and prosocial behavior. While I hope additional research in the future, both qualitative and quantitative, will add to our understanding of how reading narrative fiction can change both how a reader understands self and how he or she acts in the world, our intuitive understandings, as readers and teachers, also inform this model.

Researching Relationships Between Social Action and Literature

It appears that there is some research-based evidence that reading fiction and social action (or prosocial behavior) are linked; however, this link is tenuous at best, as the studies demonstrating this linkage are few. The reasons for this lack of

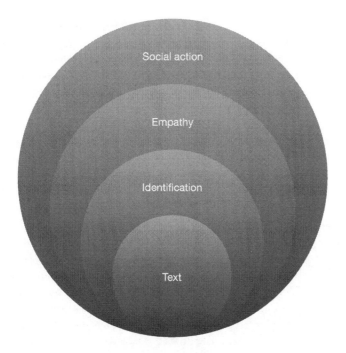

FIGURE 5.1 How reading changes behavior. As a reader engages with a text, emotional, attitudinal and behavioral changes can result, contextualizing the reading experience and extending its influence outward. Social action is the largest sphere because when actions do result from narrative experience they comprise the largest cultural context for reading.

research are many, including the challenging problems of designing an empirical study that can demonstrate a cause/effect relationship between literary reading and behavior change. How is a researcher to demonstrate the complexity inherent in the diagram above, the complexity of the cognitive/affective reading process and its effect on real-world actions? First, such a study would almost by necessity have to take place over time, and over many reading experiences and responses, and incorporate reader observation. Then, what kind of behavior change would the researcher look for to be significant? How could one behavior be isolated and examined? And how might this behavior be clearly linked to a fictional reading experience, while eliminating other variables?

There are other reasons why there have been so few studies linking reading and behavior: perhaps such a hypothesis seriously oversimplifies the personal and idiosyncratic process of experiencing narrative worlds; or perhaps such a link doesn't really exist at all. Perhaps narratives are so wrapped up with our very sense of self and who we are that we simply can't untangle all the narrative effects on our lives in a way that enables generalizations about reading literature. Perhaps the best we will be able to do is demonstrate linkages between reading and feelings, such as empathy and identification, or between reading and thinking. Or perhaps there is a way to uncover a connection.

Regardless, I think there is enough evidence, theoretical, philosophical, experiential, and/or empirical, to argue that reading fiction can change behavior in positive ways, ways that include increased helping behavior and more thoughtfully considered interactions with others. It seems likely that with engaged interactions with narrative texts, readers do more than just have temporary feelings or compulsions to imitate characters. In the paragraphs that follow, I summarize some of the most significant research to date exploring connections between reading fiction and social action.

I'll begin with research linking empathy to prosocial behaviors, with no mention of literature or reading. Eisenberg and Miller (1987) conducted a meta-analysis of research attempting to link feelings of empathy to prosocial action. While in an earlier analysis (Underwood and Moore, 1982) no relationship was found between affective empathy and prosocial behavior, Eisenberg and Miller had different results, as they found that "low to moderate positive relations generally were found between empathy and both prosocial behavior and cooperative/socially competent behavior" (p. 91).

Other research has tried to verify the next link in the chain, the one connecting reading literature first to empathy, and then to prosocial behavior. Hakemulder's (2000) meta-analysis of this research was not as optimistic as Eisenberg and Miller's was. Hakemulder summarized that "there is little empirical evidence, let alone any meta-analytic review to support this [that reading stories has behavior effects]" (p. 91). Hakemulder describes two more in-depth studies that examined the effects of reading on readers' actions. One did not find any significant changes in helping behavior after reading (Wiley, 1991), and a second (McArthur & Eisen, 1976) did find effects on behavior, but only in terms of persistence with a difficult task after reading about a high achieving character. However, while the persistent behavior observed may have been connected to the recent reading experience, this may have been primarily because the participants were directly exposed to a very similar challenge very soon after reading.

The closest research linking reading and significant social action that Hakemulder could find was that of Bilsky (1989), who found that reading stories about social dilemmas resulted in enhanced motivation for prosocial behavior, as measured on a written test (Hakemulder, p. 43). However, there was no link found between this motivation and physical actions. Otherwise, the general results of his meta-analysis were that:

> empathic arousal, at least in adults, consistently leads to prosocial action (Batson et al., 1981; Eisenberg and Miller, 1987; Hoffman, 1977). Although there is no evidence that reading stories may enhance altruistic behavior (Wiley, 1991), reading stories containing prosocial dilemmas was found to enhance motivation for prosocial behavior.
>
> *(Bilsky, 1989)*

In my own research, I found two empirical studies that made a definitive connection between reading fiction and prosocial behavior. In the first, Johnson (2012) made a link between reading fiction and subsequent affective empathy and helping behavior. His participants read a story and took a measure of affective empathy, as well as a mood assessment and a "transportation" scale (p. 151). Then, the researcher "accidently" dropped pens in front of the participants and recorded which participants helped to pick up the pens. He found that "individuals who were more transported into the story reported significantly higher affective empathy for the characters" and that:

> the hypotheses that transportation and affective empathy would translate into real-world behavior were also supported as individuals who experienced higher transportation and affective empathy were significantly more likely to help the experimenter pick up the pens.
>
> *(p. 152)*

The researcher (and author) conclude, "this is the first study, to this author's knowledge, to show a direct link between reading narrative fiction, affective empathy, and helping behavior" (p. 154).

The second study I found, conducted by Lee et al. (2014), explored whether exposure by children to a storybook providing a lesson about lying would change their lying behavior. In the study, the researcher showed the children a toy and then asked them not to turn around and peek at it while the researcher briefly left the room. Meanwhile, there was a video camera taping each child's behavior. Then, when returning, the researchers read a storybook to the child, sometimes with a theme related to lying. After the reading, the children were asked if they looked at the toy, and the researchers assessed which children lied and which story they read. The researchers found that only the children who read a story about George Washington in which the main character benefited from truth-telling were significantly less likely to lie to the researcher. They concluded that stories can affect moral behavior if young readers are exposed to a story showing the positive consequences of being good.

As the number of empirical studies explicitly linking narrative fiction reading and prosocial behavior are few, the jury may still be out on whether reading changes what people do, and, if so, if researchers can prove it. Perhaps there will be more research in the future to support what many of us know intuitively and experientially: reading changes who we are, and what we do.

The Pedagogy of Social Action

Service learning

The last specific pedagogy I will address is the pedagogy of social action, a pedagogy that, for obvious reasons, is closely linked to teaching literature to encourage social action or behavior change. Service learning is having students engage in some type of community service as part of a classroom project or investigation. In the most effective service learning there are strong curricular connections between the experience and the content of the class, as well as a truly mutual, or reciprocal partnership between the school or classroom and the community being served; in other words, both parties benefit. As has been discussed in this chapter, it is quite difficult to identify precise, definitive behavior changes that may result from reading fiction, even though several researchers have tried. Most of the time, the closest connection that can be made through research is between feelings of empathy and prosocial behavior—the literature piece is illusive. Service learning may be one way to lead students closer to prosocial action directly related to literature they may be reading and their responses to it. If the service learning has relevance and meaning, even a class assignment *requiring* students to engage in some kind of action may suffice as positive behavior change; at least it provides a model for the type of behavior or social action in which students may *choose* to engage in the future. Following the pattern of earlier chapters, I define the pedagogical concept below, connect it to social action, and, finally, return to the visual model presented earlier in this chapter to make some final comments about service learning and literature.

What is service learning?

Service learning is defined as a combination of classroom, content learning and community service. Students are actively engaged in participating within some kind of community organization, institution or program, and what they learn through this engagement supplements the learning objectives of the course in which they are enrolled. As noted earlier, the most effective service learning results in reciprocal, or mutual benefit; additionally, it must be connected to the school curriculum and allow time for students to reflect upon and respond to the partnerships in which they are engaging so that the connection makes sense (see Eyler et al., 1999). Effective service learning is not just volunteering or helping out a group in need, although such behaviors are indeed worthy civic activities. Service learning, as it is educational in nature, should be connected to learning goals or objectives, such as those that might be devised by a teacher of literature. Such goals may range from critical thinking to problem-solving and understanding how otherwise abstract issues are realized and addressed in real-world settings. Service learning has theoretical connections (as does social justice pedagogy) to the experiential work of Dewey, as well as to pragmatism, a philosophy asserting that abstract knowledge should result in a real-world function or useful action. Service learning may go one step further than pedagogies of social justice or critical pedagogy, as it explicitly asks students to engage in real-world action as part of the classroom experience; the experience is not something that the teacher hopes will happen later—it's something that is a required part of the class.

Some critique service learning on the grounds that it encourages a type of helping or assisting that can be condescending or even discriminatory if students are not properly prepared for the experience. Additionally, if the service is not adequately connected to course goals then the experience can seem like busy work or just volunteering that has no close connection to learning. When thinking of the teaching of literature, service learning might be related to issues and concepts discussed in and through a fictional text; perhaps parallels could be drawn between the experiences of characters in a book and how these experiences translate in the students' real world. Then, with service learning, students could have an outlet for helping to ameliorate problems, remove roadblocks, or resolve misunderstandings. Hence, reading literature results not only in critical thinking and critical consciousness, but ultimately ends up being a catalyst for community action and change.

Connections between service learning and the social action

As described above, service-learning pedagogy and the concept of teaching literature to encourage social action seem to have the potential to work hand-in-hand. Reading and responding to a text leads to a discovery or clarification of issues of concern or unjust (or simply unexamined) situations or sites in need of revision; then, with the help of the literature teacher, the students engage in related community service that addresses the situation in the students' very own community. Returning to the visual model of social action and literary experience presented earlier in this chapter, when reading a text, students might first identify with its characters, events and settings and then empathize with them; finally, they might be led to social action. Service learning can be just such social action.

BOX 5.1   SAMPLE LITERATURE LESSON TO ENCOURAGE SOCIAL ACTION

Contributed by Chea Parton, Purdue University, formerly of Southern Wells Community Schools, Poneto, Indiana.

Bullying and Bryce Courtenay's *The Power of One* and Jean Haversham's fictional letter, "Blue Jean"

In this unit, we've seen and discussed several types of bullying. Whether large-scale (apartheid in *The Power of One*) or small-scale bullying (in school in "Blue Jean"), it is clear that hurt people hurt people. In this project, you will explore the perspective of either someone who is bullied or someone who bullies.

The Written Portion

For this portion, select one of the following options:

The Poem

Write a poem that fulfills the following criteria:

- contains eight to ten lines and a creative title
- contains at least three examples of figurative language
- uses vivid language and description
- is written from the perspective of someone who has been bullied, who bullies others, or from bullying itself

The Letter

Write a letter that fulfills the following criteria:

- is at least one page long
- uses vivid language and description
- creates an authentic and believable voice
- is written to someone who has been bullied, encouraging them; to someone who has bullied others explaining why what they do is wrong; or to someone you have bullied, apologizing for your actions
- uses pseudonym

The Editorial

Write a persuasive editorial posing a solution to bullying at Southern Wells. It should fulfill the following criteria:

- is at least one page long with a creative title
- uses vivid language and description
- creates an authentic and persuasive voice
- poses an implementable solution to the problem (i.e., Just "be nicer to each other" is not a solution that could be implemented; holding a convocation where students can discuss the issue openly and honestly with one another is.)

Flash Fiction

Write a piece of flash fiction (a single moment) that fulfills the following criteria:

- is at least one page long with a creative title
- uses at least three examples of figurative language

- uses vivid language and description
- is written in the first person and begins in the middle of things
- does not have rising action, falling action or a resolution: it is a flash, a rendering of a single moment
- is written from the perspective of someone who has been bullied or someone who bullies. (This does not need to be from personal experience.)

The Creative Portion

This portion of the project will be completed on poster board, will contain your written portion, and also include, the following:

- at least five images that represent bullying and the emotions that come with it
- at least one quote that describes, depicts, illustrates, etc. the problems, causes and effects of bullying

Note: At the end of this project, students started an anti-bullying club at Southern Wells Junior/Senior High School.

Lesson Plan References

Courtenay, B. (1989). *The power of one*. New York: Random House.
Haversham, J. (1999). Blue Jean/Gene letter. In C.H. Weaver and J. Everly, *Personal projects: 21 projects for self discovery and celebration*. Austin, TX: Dandy Lion Publishers.

References

Adams, M., Blumenfeld, W., Castaneda, C., Hackman, H., Peters, M. & Zuniga, X. (2010). *Readings for diversity and social justice: An anthology on racism, anti-semitism, sexism, heterosexism, ableism, and classism*, 2nd edn. New York: Routledge.

Alsup, J. (2010). *Young adult literature and adolescent identity across cultures and classrooms: Contexts for the literary lives of teens*. New York: Routledge.

Apple, M. (2006). Interrupting the right: On doing crucial educational work in conservative times. In G. Ladson-Billings & W.F. Tate (Eds), *Educational research in the public interest: Social justice, action, and policy*, pp. 27–45. New York: Teachers College Press.

Ayers, W. (1998). Popular education: Teaching for social justice. In W. Ayers, J.A. Hunt, & T. Quinn (Eds), *Teaching for social justice*, pp. xvi–xxv. New York: New Press.

Batson, C.D., Duncan, B.D. & Ackerman, P. (1981). Is empathic emotion a source of altruistic motivation? *Journal of Personality and Social Psychology*, 40, 290–302.

Bender-Slack, D. (2010). Texts, talk . . . and fear? English language arts teachers negotiate social justice teaching. *English Education*, 42(2), 181–203.

Bilsky, W. (1989). *Angewandte altruismusforschung: analyse und rezeption von texten uber hilfeleistung*. Bern: Huber.

Booth, W. (1961). *The rhetoric of fiction.* Chicago: University of Chicago Press.

Bruner, J. (1986). *Actual minds, possible worlds.* Cambridge, MA: Harvard University.

Campbell, J. (1972). *Myths to live by.* New York: Viking Press.

Cochran-Smith, M. (1999). Learning to teach for social justice. In G.A. Griffin (Ed.), *The education of teachers,* pp. 114–144. Chicago: University of Chicago Press.

Cochran-Smith, M. (2004). *Walking the road: Race, diversity, and social justice in teacher education.* New York: Teachers College Press.

Crites, S. (1986). Storytime: Recollecting the past and projecting the future. In Eisenberg, N. & Miller, P.A. (1987). The relation of empathy to prosocial and related behaviors. *Psychological Bulletin,* 101(1), 91–119.

Eisenberg, N. & Miller, P.A. (1987). The relation of empathy to prosocial and related behaviors. *Psychological Bulletin,* 101, 91–119.

Eyler, J., Giles, D.E. & Astin, A.W. (1999). *Where's the learning in service-learning?.* San Francisco, CA: Jossey-Bass.

Frye, N. (1964). *The educated imagination.* Bloomington, IN: Indiana University Press.

Gerrig, R. (1993). *Experiencing narrative worlds: On the psychological activities of reading.* New Haven, CT: Yale University Press.

Hakemulder, J. (2000). *The moral laboratory: Experiments examining the effects of reading literature on social perception and moral self-concept.* Amsterdam/Philadelphia: John Benjamins.

Hoffman, M.L. (1977). Empathy: Its development and prosocial implication. In C.B. Keasey (Ed.), *Nebraska Symposium on Motivation,* 25, 169–217.

Holland, N. (2009). *Literature and the brain.* Cambridge, MA: The PsyArt Foundation.

Jahn, M. (1999). "Speak, friend, and enter": Garden paths, artificial intelligence and cognitive narratology. In D. Herman (Ed.), *Narratologies: New perspectives on narrative analysis,* pp. 167–194. Columbus: Ohio State University Press.

Johnson, D.R. (2012). Transportation into a story increases empathy, prosocial behavior, and perceptual bias toward fearful expressions. *Personality and Individual Differences,* 52, 150–155.

Lee, K., Talwar, V., McCarthy, A., Ross, I., Evans, A. & Arruda, C. (2014). Can classic moral stories promote honesty in children? *Psychological Science,* 25 (8), 1630–1636.

McArthur, L.Z. & Eisen, S.V. (1976). Achievements of male and female storybook characters as determinants of achievement behavior by boys and girls. *Journal of Personality and Social Psychology,* 33, 467–473.

Miller, s., Beliveau, L., DeStigter, T., Kirkland, D. & Rice, P. (2008). *Narratives of social justice teaching: How English teachers negotiate theory and practice between preservice and inservice spaces.* New York: Peter Lang.

Nieto, S. & Bode, P. (2011). *Affirming diversity: The sociopolitical context of multicultural education,* 6th edn. New York. Allyn & Bacon.

Polkinghorne, D.E. (1991). Narrative and self-concept. *Journal of Narrative and Life History,* 1(2&3), 135–153.

Runciman, W.G. (Ed.) (1978). *Max Weber: Selections in translation.* E. Matthews, trans. Cambridge, MA: Cambridge University Press.

Underwood, B. & Moore, B. (1982). Perspective-taking and altruism. *Psychological Bulletin,* 91, 143–173.

Wiley, L.S. (1991). *Impact of story-based and problem-solving character education on altruistic behavior in the preschool classroom.* PhD Diss. Boston, MA: Boston College.

Wortham, S. (2001). *Narratives in action: A strategy for research and analysis.* New York: Teachers College Press.

PART II
Challenges to Literary Study

My perceptions of the challenges to literary study are what made this book happen. These challenges present and visible in US policy and politics, and even in the attitudes and expectations of the citizenry, have created a climate of consumerism, accountability, and standardization, all of which can undermine the liberal arts and the humanistic methods of literature teachers. However, we must understand the challenges if we are to meet them.

Becoming a Reader

I was in 7th grade when I decided that I was done with *Fear Street* and horse novels. I wanted to read "classics." I wasn't sure what "classics" actually were, but I had become convinced that all adults read classics—though my own parents preferred Grisham, King, and Irving. I received *The Count of Monte Cristo*, *The Jungle*, and *1984* for my birthday. I read *The Jungle* first, not entirely understanding why everyone was attending socialist meetings when there were giant man-eating rats on the loose. *1984* was easier. I'd read some sci-fi and dystopian young adult fiction, and I felt like I understood what was being said through story in a way that I couldn't through the oration and exposition in *The Jungle*. I'd saved *The Count of Monte Cristo* for last because of sheer length and the difficult vocabulary on the first page alone, but my pre-teen brain quickly became enraptured with the escape, elaborate revenge plots, and unrequited love. The ending, though, is what changed my reading tastes forever. I expected the good guy to win his love and defeat his enemy. Instead, the book's conclusion was about regret, about guilt, about forgiveness, about the meaning of justice. I felt immensely sad for the count, and satisfied too.

All three texts confirmed that I could access "adult" ideas; they sparked within me a desire for books that challenged my expectations for plot, character, and happy endings. I learned that readerly satisfaction wasn't just about winning the race or catching the murderer, but about empathizing with other—albeit fictional— people and considering my own humanity. Now, I write fiction with the hope that my characters—no matter how flawed— will invite the readers to think and feel, like Dantes, like Winston and Julia, like Jurgis.

By Natalie Lund

Reading Snapshot

The snapshot I chose to write about occurred right before I started high school. Before then, I never read for fun. I read for AR (accelerated reader) in grade school and read the in-class assignments in junior high, but I never felt like reading was a fun thing. It always seemed like a burden.

The summer before high school was very stressful for me. I was switching schools and didn't know anyone in my area. I was very close with my cousin through this time because she was the only person my age who I knew about. Some point over that summer, my mom picked up a book from the store that she thought I might like. I never even tried to read the book, so I let my cousin borrow it. She finished the book in two days and would not stop talking about how good it was. She convinced me to read the book, *The Sisterhood of the Traveling Pants*.

I fell in love with the book and finished it in only a few days. My mom was shocked because I had never read a book before that I wasn't required to read. Within a couple of weeks I had finished all four books in the series. When I finished reading the last book, I could have cried. I wanted to keep on reading about this incredible group of friends and the connection they had over these magical pants they found.

Since then, I have only read a couple of books. I always feel like I need to read more often, but I never am able to bring myself to make time to read for fun I hope I will be able to learn to make time very soon because I really would love to get lost in a good book like I did back before high school.

By Lydia Ann Drenth

Reference

Brashares, A. (2003). *Sisterhood of the traveling pants*. New York: Random House.

6

LITERATURE CURRICULUM AND STANDARDS-BASED EDUCATION

> Discussions of curriculum in American schools and colleges have usually focused
> on what is most worth knowing: Should we stress the Great Books, the richness
> of multiculturalism, the basic literacy needed in the worlds of work and leisure?
> But these arguments have been based on false premises and reflect a fundamental
> misconception of the nature of knowing.
>
> *(Applebee, A.N., 1996, p. 3)*

When I became a high school English teacher in 1990, I had little idea what was
meant by curriculum. I began teaching in a small, rural school, and there was no
published, bound, or even informally discussed English language arts curriculum
passed along to me when I took the job, unless you count the literature textbook,
which was arranged either by genre or theme in middle school, or by historical or
literary period, often within the constraints of geography (American or British
literature), in the high school grades. So the textbook *was* basically the literature
curriculum, even though I doubt I would have described it that way at the
time, and I sometimes deviated from its offerings. Additionally, I was given the
impression that colleagues and administrators expected a traditional approach to
the teaching of these selections, focusing on teacher-provided "meanings" and
teacher-led question and answer sessions about important aspects of the texts.
Since that time, I have learned much about the various ways in which a literature
curriculum can be structured and how these varieties may affect student learning.
Now I understand that despite the goals of many publishing companies, textbooks
and curriculum are not synonymous, nor should they be.

Part II of this book is devoted to challenges to teaching and learning literature,
how recent ideologies and policies surrounding secondary education have led to
the marginalization of subjective, emotive, or locally relevant learning in favor of

objective and standardized teaching and learning that is easily assessable and countable. This chapter outlines some of these challenges as they are connected to the historical views of literature curriculum in the secondary school. First, I provide an overview of secondary literature curriculum as I understand its evolution, focusing on theories of curriculum from the 1980s to the present. Of course, literature curriculum has been influenced by notions of standardization and accountability, notions that began to be popular in the '80s and have continued to retain significance, if in a modified way. Therefore, I spend the second part of this chapter discussing the notion of standards-based education in the US and how it has specifically affected the teaching of literature, compounding the challenges to literary study valuing aesthetic and reader response. I end the chapter with an overview of where we currently are in disciplinary thinking about the literature curriculum and how current theory and research may conflict with simultaneous trends toward increased standardization, accountability, corporate models of education, and regimentation.

The Evolution of Literature Curriculum

Arthur Applebee writes that the literature curriculum as we know it was born in the late 19th century (1993, p. 23). In those early days, literature was seen as a source of moral lessons and a way to transmit cultural values, with pedagogical techniques focusing on rote memorization, teacher-led "discussions," and directives to find the hidden meanings of texts, which only the teachers seemed to know. New Critical close readings, historical approaches to teaching literature, and focus on canonical texts were the norm, both at the secondary and post secondary levels. This way of teaching literature basically viewed literary texts as rhetorical products of great thinkers, whose words students were to memorize, regurgitate, and model.

This pattern of literature teaching persisted for quite a long time, and aspects of it, such as historical approaches and focus on canonical texts, continue today, as often seen in textbook organization and school text selections (Applebee 1992, 1993). However, the literature curriculum in secondary schools in the US began to become more diversified in the 1970s, and educational scholars began writing voraciously about creative approaches to the literature curriculum in the 80s and 90s, with the increased popularity and notoriety of response-based and workshop-based approaches (see Purves et al., 1972/1994; Atwell, 1987/1998; Beach and Marshall, 1990).

Why it took so long for these changes and innovations to begin is unclear; perhaps muddy notions of what the English curriculum should look like attributed to this stagnancy, or perhaps traditional, patriarchal ideas of which texts are valuable had something to do with it. However, when schools of thoughts such as feminism, Marxism, critical race studies, reader response theory and cultural studies became players in the university curriculum in the '70s and '80s, new secondary school teachers began their teaching careers with broadened notions of what is considered real literature, books worthy of student reading and study. Regardless, and as Applebee's study (1993) showed us, there has been tremendous stability in which texts high school English teachers and schools choose for study over time (Applebee, 1996, p. 28), with focus still being on canonical texts such as Shakespearean plays and books including *Huckleberry Finn*, *The Scarlet Letter*, and *The Great Gatsby*. One has to wonder if the results would be much different if a similar survey of teachers was conducted today.

In the late 1990s and 2000s these student-centered, multicultural approaches to teaching literature continued to grow and become richer, with the work of Allen Carey-Webb connecting literature teaching to cultural studies (2001), Richard Beach, Deborah Appleman, Susan Hynds, and Jeffrey Wilhelm (2006) exploring literature teaching through the lenses of social/cultural issues and response-based approaches, Sheridan Blau's (2003) extension of the concept of workshop approaches to the teaching of literature, and both Appleman's (2000) and Lisa Schade Eckert's (2006) discussions of how literary theory can be used as cultural-social lenses through which to understand literary texts. Most recently, Beach et al. (2012) described an approach to literature teaching which they coined a "literacy practices approach," an approach which "substitutes the idea of literacy practices for skills, practices whose meaning are grounded in social contexts" (p. 23), thereby making the literary experience locally relevant to students. In looking at the movement in notions of literature curriculum over time, it is easy to see the trend moving away from singular attention to the text, to focus on social/cultural contexts, and then back to a more centered approach where the text is still the object of study, but is also read as a window into locally relevant issues. In the section that follows, I discuss various literature curricular frameworks or categories based on the work of the English education scholars noted above.

Major Literature Curriculum Frameworks

Based on the work of the English education and literacy theorists, scholars and pedagogues briefly described above, I briefly outline and describe here various key literature teaching curricular frameworks from the 1990s to the present. Many of these frameworks can trace their origins to much earlier approaches or theories, but have evolved in the last twenty to thirty years to take on increased relevance for secondary school teachers.

The response-based approach

Response-based literature curricula, such as that advocated by Alan Purves et al. (1972/1994) and Arthur Applebee (1996), grew from the reader response theories of scholars such as Rosenblatt (1938/1978) and Bleich (1978). While the reader response theorists focus on the act of reading, the curricular scholars and pedagogues focus on how to translate these understandings about the act of reading to teaching literature. (Note: Rosenblatt played both roles.) If we believe that the act of reading is a transaction, and the reader brings to a text knowledge and experience which affect its meaning, then we should teach literature by honoring the student reader's response. While this does not mean that any and all responses are equally informed or relevant, it does mean that the teacher attempts to elicit response, to draw from students their thoughts, responses, and questions during reading, interpretation, and even criticism. This type of curriculum often relies heavily on classroom discussion, or "conversation" (Applebee, 1996, p. 3). The teacher structures classroom discussions that attempt to invite student response, dialogues about various responses, and even debates about conflicting opinions. Many of the other frameworks below integrate response-based teaching as part of their ideology.

The thematic or integrated approach

This approach is perhaps most often seen at the middle school level, when textbooks are even organized by theme (e.g., "friendship," "family") rather than historical period or genre. However, any level of literature teacher can structure a literature curriculum about themes or issues, and then choose literature that fits within these themes. Therefore, the focus of the instruction becomes making connections to the themes and how the texts contribute to understandings of these themes. In this way, teachers hope students will find the literature more relevant and interesting. Closely related is the next category, cultural studies or sociocultural approaches. A good example of the thematic approach was focused on the university level, when literary theorist and humanist Gerald Graff (1993, p. 15) proposed "teaching the conflicts" around academic issues and literary studies, in addition to teaching the literature itself. Another example more focused on secondary English education can be found in Smagorinsky and Gevinson (1989) who lay out a scope and sequence for a thematic literature curriculum grades 7–12 that includes focus on affective, as well as cognitive, response.

Cultural studies or sociocultural approaches

Cultural studies or sociocultural approaches to literature teaching focus on cultural and social issues and concerns and include literature that speaks to these issues in various ways. Issues such as gender stereotyping, racism, poverty, violence, and homophobia are cultural and social issues about which much literature is written, or on which much literature at least comments. In this approach, popularized by Rick Beach et al. (2006) and Allen Carey-Webb (2001) among others, teachers ask students to think about key concerns or ideologies in their own communities, to read and respond to related literary texts, and think about how these texts might inform real-life issues and the readers' responses to them. Here literature is seen as both a reflection of society and a living organism, which can speak back to readers and communities, particularly when readers' responses are solicited and students are allowed to grapple with the ideas and issues that literature confronts and explores. So in a sense, reading becomes a gateway to social activism.

The workshop-based approach

Again, as many of these theories are not mutually exclusive, workshop-based approaches often incorporate response, thematic organization, and cultural criticism. However workshop-based approaches do all this in small groups, or student workshop groups. Nancie Atwell's famous *In the Middle: New Understandings about Writing, Reading, and Learning* (1987/1998) was perhaps the first popular text to practically discuss how and why to organize a middle-school class around a so-called workshop approach, which allows students to read independently, work on individual reading projects, respond and discuss in small groups, and make choices about what to read. Blau's 2003 book continues the discussion of how to teach reading and literature through the workshop approach, which he defines as focusing "at least as much on the process of reading and producing discourse about literature as it is on the substance of the discourse produced" (p. 13). In other words, teachers and students together discuss literature, responses to it, connections with it, and questions about how to best read it. In many ways, the response-based approach to the literature curriculum capitalizes on the very successful National Writing Project model for teaching writing.

The literary theory-based approach

In the early to mid-2000s, great interest was generated by Deborah Appleman's *Critical Encounters in High School English: Teaching Literary Theory to Adolescents* (2000) in explicitly teaching various literary theories to high school students to help them think about literary texts. Appleman, and later Eckert (2006), argue that the teaching of theories such as feminism, Marxism, deconstruction, and postmodernism can help students understand that academic and sociocultural lenses can be applied to literary texts to facilitate their reading—and even to read and understand texts in different ways. Consequently, literary theory, and the reading of literary texts, might be demystified. Theory-based approaches rely heavily on cultural or sociocultural approaches to the curriculum, as well as response-based approaches. They also require a fair amount of close reading.

The literacy practices approach

Last, I want to talk briefly about the literacy practices approach advocated in 2012 by Beach, Thein and Webb. In their book, *Teaching to Exceed the English Language*

Arts Common Core State Standards: A Literacy Practices Approach for 6-12 Classrooms, they argue that teaching ELA as a set of contextualized literacy practices with real-world significance, as opposed to a set of decontextualized and transferable skills, can increase student motivation and learning. They say such an approach allows students to "frame events, construct identities, collaborate with others, synthesize and create texts, and use 21st-century tools in complex, multimodal ways" (p. viii). Clearly this approach, which encourages teachers to create "affinity spaces" (p. viii) for students through thematic units, incorporates cultural studies-based and response-based activities that connect literature to issues in a student's community, school, or family. The literacy practices approach also advocates the use of technology and multimedia, as these are the communicative conduits of adolescents.

Given the argument of this book with its focus on subjective knowledge, emotional response, and even motivation for behavior change after reading literature, many of these approaches have the potential to be quite effective. Asking students to respond personally and critically, to talk to others about their responses and interpretations, and connect their readings to real life, seem to be useful approaches and activities that might enhance the reading experience and expand its relevance. By connecting literature to what is important to them and their peers, students are probably identifying and empathizing with events and characters, which helps them to understand themselves and others more deeply. They are reading and responding to narrative texts, and thinking critically about them, but also considering what the story can teach them in a world increasingly dominated by unfiltered information, intolerance, and an epidemic of lack of compromise.

The Standards-based Movement and Literature Teaching

Standards-based education in the US has affected all aspects of the teaching of English language arts in the secondary school, and literature teaching is no exception. But what exactly is meant by standards-based education? The Rand Corporation (2008) defines "standards-based reforms" as including "academic expectations for students," "alignment of key elements of the educational system," "use of assessments of student achievement," "decentralization of responsibility for decisions relating to curriculum," "support and technical assistance to foster improvement of educational services," and "accountability provisions that reward or sanction schools or students on the basis of measured performance" (p. 2). These characteristics are connected to political and policy trends in the US, as well as to changing attitudes toward teachers among the general populace; in short, teachers are not as trusted, and it is a growing belief that both schools and teachers need to be monitored closely to ensure quality instruction. Hamilton et al. (2012) of the Rand Corporation, write that there are both positive and negative consequences of the standards movement; one of their most interesting conclusions concerns the conflation of standards and testing, which often ends up being "high stakes" for students and teachers:

> The preponderance of research on the impact of testing rather than the impact of standards reflects the emerging realisation [*sic*] that "standards-based accountability" has largely given way to "test-based accountability," a system in which the test rather than the standards communicates expectations and drives practice.
>
> *(p. 159)*

Standards alone do not improve education, and testing is not equivalent to learning—or good teaching.

Most sources locate the beginning of the standards movement in the '80s during Ronald Reagan's presidency, although there were earlier hints of more government regulation of education, including the 1965 passage of the Elementary and Secondary Education Act and the 1972 passage of the Education of All Handicapped Children Act. In the Cold War era of the '80s, there was increased insecurity about safety and keeping America's competitive edge with Russia, China, and Cuba. Hence increased attention was paid to academic standards and teacher/school accountability. In fact, it was during this time that the word "standards" was probably first used ubiquitously about elementary and secondary education. In the early '80s, with the conservative Reagan presidency, attention to standards skyrocketed, as did discussions of the accountability of schools and teachers. There was an increased belief that schools needed to justify and explain their approaches if they were to receive federal funding, and business models of K–12 education were in their infancy—what do we need to *input* in order to get the appropriate *output* of student learning? In 1983, the publication of *A Nation at Risk: The Imperative for Educational Reform* was a catalyst for further change, as the book argued, "America's economic security would be severely compromised" (Nichols and Berliner, 2007, p. 4) if something wasn't changed in K–12 education. The publication relied on comparisons of American school children's test results with those of children in other countries, which showed US children to be lagging behind. These numbers were later shown to be flawed. (Berliner and Biddle, 1996). *A Nation at Risk* resulted in an increased attention to standards, "higher" standards, and more educator accountability, compounding the assumption that teachers are somehow to blame for low student performance. In 2001, the G.W. Bush presidency successfully passed the next key piece of legislation in the history of the standards movement, a re-authorization of the Elementary and Secondary Education Act called *No Child Left Behind* (NCLB). This act required accountability through standardized testing and the resultant ranking and labeling of schools and districts; if scores were too low, schools could be re-organized or even closed. Most recently, the Obama administration has given dozens of waivers to states that have not been able to meet the unrealistic and punitive expectations of NCLB, yet replaced it with their own version of educational reform called *Race to the Top*, which provides access to federal funding for states that adopt the Common Core State Standards and related educator evaluation and accountability policies, and even, potentially, linked assessments aligned with the CCSS. Standards-based policies and related emphases on educator accountability are alive and well in the US in the 21st century.

What's the Challenge, and Where do We Go From Here?

So how have standards-based approaches and policies affected the literature curriculum in the secondary school, and, by association, the literary experiences of adolescents? As with all disciplines, English teachers have been increasingly pressed to raise student scores on standardized assessments both to improve their school's ranking and their own chances for merit pay (not to mention increasing student learning, which seems to have been forgotten in the mix). To do this, teachers often feel as though they must adhere very closely to the standards in the standards documents, whether the CCSS or another state-approved set, and train their students how to successfully take the tests—so test taking becomes a skill added to the curriculum. And the curriculum itself is often modified to more closely imitate the standards as stated in the policy documents, standards that can focus on transferable, measurable, and decontextualized skills, as they are easier to identify, assess, and compare across schools, districts, states, and even nations. Below, I summarize what I see as the major challenges to literature curriculum and literary study posed by standards-based education and often related high stakes assessments.

The scripted curriculum

The scripted curriculum is a curriculum that is designed and packaged by publishing companies for teaching use, often with accompanying, explicit instructions for how teachers should deliver the lessons, including pacing, activities, topics, expected student responses, and even precise scripts for teachers to read. Such scripted curricula are seen by some as useful for struggling readers who need more basic skills instruction (Davis, 2009). While scripted curricula, particularly reading curricula such as Open Court, are mostly found in the primary grades, others are also created for secondary readers as well, including Corrective Reading (SRA McGraw-Hill) and Read 180 (Scholastic). In 2008, The National Council of Teachers of English (NCTE) passed a "resolution on scripted curricula" which states, in part, that NCTE will "oppose policies that require educators to utilize scripted programs and materials" based on the belief that "NCTE must reaffirm the authority of teachers as professionals who should make the decisions regarding materials and practices in literacy education" (www. ncte.org/positions/statements/scriptedcurricula). Scripted curricula, by its very definition, forestalls any exploratory conversation and spontaneous personal reader response, aspects of literature teaching that I have argued in this book are essential for meaningful narrative experience.

National curriculum

Throughout this book, I've mentioned the CCSS, the standards currently adopted by forty-four states plus the District of Columbia, which are the closest our nation has ever come to a set of "national" standards. However, standards and curriculum are very different things, and even with the adoption of standards, and eventually aligned exams, teachers and schools could hypothetically still devise their own curricula and daily lesson plans—in other words, how the standards are taught could still be controlled locally. However, this separation between standards and curriculum may be at risk. In March 2011, the Pearson Corporation and the Bill and Melinda Gates Foundation teamed up to begin the creation of twenty-four common courses for math and English, four of which will be available free online, while the entire set will be available for purchase from Pearson Corporation (Gewertz, 2011). It's hard to tell where such efforts will go, and how many states, teachers, and schools will actually be affected, but the trend toward a national, common curricula sounds suspiciously similar to scripted curricula, with every teacher doing, and saying, the same thing each day. Such a standardization of the curriculum runs the risk of taking away teacher and local decision-making over daily classroom decisions. Since all communities are not the same and all students are not the same, such common curricula run the risk of ignoring diversity and place-specific needs. Literary study might be especially in danger with the Pearson–Gates curriculum and others like it as it is aligned with the CCSS, which, as I discussed in the Introduction, have down-played literary study in the secondary grades in favor of the reading and writing of nonfiction and expository texts and the teaching of "transferable" skills that might be taught with shorter excerpts rather than lengthy narratives which require more class time.

Quantification of the literary experience

As I've tried to argue throughout this book, the experiences of literary reading and the narrative experience, cognitive and affective, are based in subjective, emotive, and locally relevant reading and response. Responses such as identification, empathy, and being moved to social action are not easily countable or assessable through standardized, machine-scored assessments. They are also not easily comparable across readers, schools, states or nations, as the thoughts, feelings, opinions, and questions that arise during a transaction with a fictional text, and subsequent conversations with peers and teachers, may vary from person to person, context to context, text to text. While it is possible, and may be desirable, to identify the thinking and reading skills that are essential to rich narrative experiences such as making comparisons, connections, inferences, predictions, or asking questions, how these behaviors are elicited and enacted differs across readers, texts, and contexts. By their very nature, standards, particularly narrowly written ones, and standardized tests and curricula, strive for sameness across classrooms and numerical comparability across students, place, and time. Such calculations are inconsistent with the goals of literary study as seen in all of the disciplinary curriculum frameworks summarized earlier in this chapter and, I assume, with the goals of most ELA teachers working in secondary schools today and the English teacher educators preparing them.

Dehumanization of the humanities

This last item is connected to the previous point about quantification, so I will say little more about it here except to note that narrative experience is not only about learning skills and outcomes that can be measured and used to compare students and schools and place them in a hierarchy of success. Reading and responding to literature is about thinking, feeling, considering, guessing, predicting, wondering, and imagining. It takes time and human interaction. It does require certain reading skills, but these skills are heightened and transformed in the process. Truncating or simplifying the reading experience to make it faster, more efficient, and easier to evaluate will only succeed in draining it of its power.

References

Applebee, A.N. (1992). Stability and change in the high school canon. *English Journal*, 81, 27–32.

Applebee, A.N. (1993). *Literature in the secondary school: Studies of curriculum and instruction in the United States*. Research Monograph No. 25. Urbana, Ill: National Council of Teachers of English.

Applebee, A.N. (1996). *Curriculum as conversation: Transforming traditions of teaching and learning*. Chicago: University of Chicago Press.

Appleman, D. (2000). *Critical encounters in high school English: Teaching literary theory to adolescents*. New York and Urbana, Ill: Teachers College Press and NCTE.

Atwell, N. (1987/1998). *In the middle: New understandings about writing, reading, and learning*, 2nd edn. Portsmouth, NH: Heinemann.

Beach, R. & Marshall, J. (1990). *Teaching literature in the secondary school*. Independence, KY: Wadsworth.

Beach, R., Appleman, D., Hynds, S. & Wilhelm, J. (2006). *Teaching literature to adolescents*. Mahwah, NJ: Lawrence Erlbaum.

Beach, R., Thein, A.H. & Webb, A. (2012). *Teaching to exceed the English language arts common core state standards: A literacy practices approach for 6–12 classrooms*. New York: Routledge.

Berliner, D.C. & Biddle, B.J. (1996). *The manufactured crisis: Myths, fraud, and the attack on America's public schools*. New York: Basic Books.

Blau, S.D. (2003). *The literature workshop: Teaching texts and their readers.* Portsmouth, NH: Heinemann.

Bleich, D. (1978). *Subjective criticism.* Baltimore, MD: Johns Hopkins University Press, 1981.

Carey-Webb, A. (2001). *Literature and lives: A response-based, cultural studies approach to teaching English.* Urbana, Ill: NCTE.

Davis, H.S. (2009). Reading the script: How students and teachers understand reading in the context of a scripted intervention class. *American Reading Forum Annual Yearbook,* vol. 29, online.

Eckert, L.S. (2006). *How does it mean? Engaging reluctant readers through literary study.* Portsmouth, NH: Heinemann.

Gewertz, C. (2011). Gates, Pearson partner to craft common-core curricula. *Education Week,* April 27. Retrieved from www.edweek.org/ew/articles/2011/04/27/30pearson.h30.html

Graff, G. (1993). *Beyond the culture wars: How teaching the conflicts can revitalize American education.* New York: W.W. Norton.

Hamilton, L.S., Stecher, B.M. & Yuan, K. (2008). *Standards-based reform in the United States: History, research, and future directions.* Paper commissioned by the Center on Education Policy, Washington, DC.

Hamilton, L.S., Stecher, B.M. & Yuan, K. (2012). Standards-based accountability in the United States: Lessons learned and future directions. *Education Inquiry,* 3(2), 149–170.

Holland, N. (1968/1975). *The dynamics of literary response.* New York: W.W. Norton and Company.

Nichols, S.L. & Berliner, D.C. (2007). *Collateral damage: How high-stakes testing corrupts America's schools.* Cambridge, MA: Harvard Education Press.

Purves, A.C., Rogers, T. & Soter, A.O. (1972/1994). *How porcupines make love III: Readers, texts, cultures in the response-based literature classroom,* 2nd edn. Boston, MA: Allyn and Bacon.

Rand Corporation (2008). *Standards-based reform in the United States: History, research, and future directions.* Washington, DC: The Center on Education Policy.

Rosenblatt, L. (1938/1978). *The reader, the text, the poem: The transactional theory of the literary work.* Carbondale: Southern Illinois University Press.

Smagorinsky, P. & Gevinson, S. (1989). *Fostering the reader's response: Rethinking the literature curriculum.* Palo Alto, CA: Dale Seymour Publications.

7

CASE STUDY

College Town Middle School

Janet Alsup, Taylor Norman, and Tiffany Sedberry

In the spring of 2013, the three of us conducted a study[1] into the literary experiences of 7th and 8th grade students at a local school. We wanted to explore many of the theories presented in this book by enacting them in a real-world, school setting. Namely, we were interested in discovering whether the students' expressions of empathy intensified with the reading and study of literature, specifically narrative fiction, and subsequent written or oral response.

Our plan was to collaborate with four teachers to develop assignments to encourage empathetic responses to texts and to observe these lessons being taught. Finally, we would keep copies of student work to examine for evidence of how and when such empathetic responses occurred. Then, with the addition of a pre- and post-test using a previously validated empathy survey, including Likert scale questions such as "my friend's emotions don't affect me much," "I get caught up in other people's feelings easily," and "I often become sad when watching sad things on TV or in films" (Jolliffe & Farrington, 2006), we could see what kind of growth in empathetic feeling/response actually happened after reading and responding to fictional narratives.

After co-creating the lessons and activities, which the teachers taught and to which students responded, we found little evidence from the quantitative empathy surveys that the students' self-identified empathetic feelings increased. We were left frustrated—why didn't we see any growth in empathy, as reported on the scale? Why were student responses to the written assignments so sparse in terms of affective reactions and expressions of identification or empathy for characters or situations? Did this mean that reading the literature didn't change

---

1 A Seed Grant from Purdue's College of Education funded our project.

these students in any way, contrary to so many of the other studies and theoretical treatises cited earlier in this book? Or was something else going on?

Of course, there could be many reasons for our failure to either elicit or observe empathetic response, or so-called "social imagination", on the part of our young readers, despite the fact that teachers were teaching lessons explicitly asking them to respond in these ways. Perhaps the number of lessons we created and that the teachers taught were simply too few, or the teaching methods used were not effective, or students came to these lessons with pre-formed biases toward literature or reading that created an emotional and intellectual barrier. Perhaps the empathy scale itself, although externally validated, did not access the types of responses students were experiencing (see Jolliffe & Farrington, 2006). These were all possibilities.

We initially became interested in this study for a number of reasons—first, we are interested in intersections between cognitive science and the teaching and learning of literature, and one of the areas of great interest in cognitive science right now is how fictional literature can affect feelings and expressions of empathy, or social imagination. Second, in the middle school grades, children and adolescents often struggle both with learning to be effective readers *and* with the ability to understand themselves and others, as students in the middle grades are often moving through concrete to abstract thought (in Piaget's terms), beginning to be able to imagine the "other" rather than being limited to the world they can immediately see, hear and feel. We wondered if through narrative literature, young adolescents might be able increase their understandings of the thoughts, feelings, and intentions of others—in other words, their theory of mind. Since, as we've seen earlier, brain chemistry can change when a reader experiences fictional narrative, might it be possible that through narrative experience, and explicit guidance to consider the experiences of fictional characters, young people might be better equipped to deal with difference, diversity, and otherness? To go a step further, might fictional experience even alleviate problems such as bullying, discrimination and lack of civil discourse, which can seem rampant in the middle years? (see Miller et al., 2013). Through imagining the thoughts, feelings and intentions of characters in fictional texts, could young readers become more empathetic and tolerant of others in their own lives? That's what we really wanted to find out and, of course, what we wanted to see happen. The results, however, were a little different.

We believe the collaboration between teacher and educational researcher has the potential to create knowledge about the classroom that combines the professional with the practical. With this belief as our foundation, we hoped our work would shed light on a possible relationship between students, texts, and empathy. Because the quantitative survey suggested there was no light to shine, we decided that student work and teacher interviews might provide a qualitative set of data that *could* illuminate. As participants in this particular study, the teachers made instructional choices in order to encourage empathic reactions to fictional events as students responded through writing prompts, constructing poems and narrating personal experiences. The students' responses served as translations of their interior experiences empathizing with characters and situations in texts. The transcription and analysis of the teachers' interviews elucidated their reactions to and reflections upon their classroom experiences. This qualitative approach to understanding literature instruction and its subsequent effect ultimately illuminated the very condition of being a teacher teaching in today's educational climate, or, by association, a student trying to learn in that same environment.

College Town Middle School

College Town Middle School is a pseudonym for a 7–8th grade school in Central Indiana. It has an enrollment of approximately 1,000 students and is relatively diverse, with 60 percent Caucasian, 12 percent African American, and 20 percent Hispanic students, according to its website, accessed in May of 2014. Seventy percent of the students participate in the free or reduced federal lunch program, signaling low to average socio-economic status. We worked with four teachers, three 8th grade English teachers and one 7th grade English teacher, all of whom had taught at the school for at least three years.

In previous years, the school had struggled with standardized test scores, but at the time of this study these had risen due to hard work by the staff prompted by some bad publicity caused by a low "grade" awarded by the state as part of Indiana's "A–F accountability" program (Indiana Department of Education, 2011). In 2012, College Town Middle School received a D, and in 2013 a B. However, it is important to note that in 2011–2012 the state revised its school grading model to "improve transparency" (see website cited above) after a scandal surrounding the former state secretary of education Tony Bennett and his staff's seemingly preferential grade change for a charter school championed by Bennett.

In 2013 when we conducted this study the staff was deep in curriculum revision to align their lessons to the new Common Core State Standards (CCSS), which, at that time, Indiana had adopted (in 2014 they decided to drop the CCSS and adopt their own standards instead). The English faculty members at each grade level met regularly to discuss their lessons, align them to the standards, revise them when necessary, and make sure all teachers were addressing the CCSS. Since it was spring at the time of the study, teachers were also preparing for the state standardized exam (in Indiana called the ISTEP) and therefore had a difficult time including new or previously unplanned lessons, activities, or texts in their curriculum. Adding new literary texts, even short fiction, was a challenge, unless the text could be explicitly linked to another unit, lesson, or standard that needed to be taught. Adding additional whole novels was impossible, as the one novel in the 8th grade curriculum was already taught in the fall of the 8th grade— Lois Lowry's *The Giver* (1993)—and no novels were regularly included in the 7th grade curriculum.

"I would rather have a creative writing response or an activity . . . as opposed to just answering questions": Student responses to the assignments

The pre/post empathy survey administered to thirty-one 8th grade students who returned the requisite permission forms resulted in no statistically significant increase (or decrease) in how the students expressed empathy either cognitively (i.e., through thoughtful consideration) or affectively (i.e., through emotional contagion). However, in three of the four classes there was a total of six students who made what we call "big moves" on the empathy scale, jumping up at least ten points on the scale's quantitative measurement of either cognitive, affective, or "overall" empathetic responses to the Likert scale scenarios, indicating that the quantity of their self-reported empathetic responses increased.

Looking at the work of these students specifically, we were able to determine through qualitative analysis a commonality among the written responses of the students who increased their expressions of empathy toward others after the classroom literary experiences and subsequent responses. In short, the students who reported the most growth in their theory of mind, or social imagination, were those who responded to the stories with other stories, or who engaged in so-called imaginative responses, such as narrative or poetry, to the assigned texts.

Imaginative response, as theorized by Knoeller (2003) is a type of "voicing" of the text or "assuming textual voices," a process that "provides a vehicle for engaging imaginatively with the 'inner lives' of characters, as well as relationships among them" (p. 44). Through creative response, personal and critical response can be heightened. We hypothesized that perhaps the students who both *read* stories and *wrote* stories or poems were the most likely to report feeling increased empathy toward others expressing strong emotions.

Ms. Madison, also a pseudonym as are all teacher names referenced here, preferred more interactive assignments for her students, rather than worksheet driven, objective responses, as the quote from her states at the beginning of this section. During this study, she asked her students to write two literary texts (a poem and a narrative) in response to two fictional texts, a short story by Gary Soto, "Born Worker" (2006, from the collection *Petty Crimes*) and a narrative essay, "The Closet" by S.L. Wisenberg (2002, from the collection *Holocaust Girls*) with the intent of helping students empathize with characters and settings that might otherwise be unfamiliar to them (i.e., being a young, Mexican boy who learned a lesson about his father and a Jewish girl with ancestors in the Holocaust). The poem students wrote was a "character poem" or "I am" poem in which the student takes the perspective of one of the characters in "Born Worker," Arnie, Jose, or Mr. Clemens. Two of the "big movers" chose to write from the perspective of Mr. Clemens, the old man in the Soto story who falls, hits his head, and must be helped by Jose and Arnie. This was perhaps an unusual choice for 12- or 13-year-old middle-school students. It would have seemed more likely that they would have chosen to write from the perspective of one of the teens in the story. Regardless, these two students stepped out of their subjective comfort zones and put themselves in the shoes of an elderly man with only a toy poodle for company. Here are excerpts from what they wrote:

> *Mr. Clemens*
> I am Serious and Perfect
> I wonder why two boys showed instead of one
> I hear the loud boy aping and the other working
> I see progress from the boy that works
> I want perfection from my requests.
> I am Serious and Perfect

And

> *Mr. Clemens*
> I am deaf and old
> I wonder how long my life will be
> I hear nothing without my hearing aid
> I see Jose working hard and Arnie supervising
> I want a new poodle and hearing aid
> I am deaf and old.

These two students *became* Mr. Clemens in a way and experimented with what it must feel like to be old and fragile, within the imaginative space of a poem—even if it is a rather confined poetic form. Perhaps the pre-set form of the "I am" poem was even helpful to the identification or empathetic response, as Knoeller writes, "by relaxing sentence syntax and other prose conventions such as punctuation, poetry frees students to focus on compression of language and thought as well as heightened attention to sound" (2003, p. 46). By focusing on stated and implied images such as sights and sounds, the identification process seemed intensified.

The same intensification happened in their narrative responses to "The Closet," a fictionalized memoir with many literary characteristics, including dialogue, figurative language and character development. Ms. Madison's assignment for this narrative read as follows, in part:

> Anne Frank often wrote short stories in her diary and would share them with her family/friends in hiding for entertainment. Your task is to use all the classic short story writing elements and create a story that involves a character who experiences empathy for someone else.
> We read in "The Closet" that the main character/narrator stopped playing "Nazi" after she started to grow up and see the sadness behind the game. Her empathy for others and the situation helped her to realize that millions

of people had suffered due to the real Nazis during the time of WWII and the Holocaust.

You should put yourself in the main character's shoes as you write this story. It should have a beginning, where you introduce the main characters and part of the basic situation, a middle, and conclusion or closing paragraph where the character realizes the error of his/her ways or a character makes someone else realize the error of his/her ways. (March 2013)

Here's how, in part, the students responded:

Last summer, my friend told me some bad news. Her dad found a job in Vancouver, and she had to move.

"I understand your pain," I told her, "but you know you should stay with your family."

She took a sign and said, "I know, but I've grown up here. This is my home. This is where I'm from. This is all I know."

I sighed and let out the ever famous words, "Sometimes the hardest thing and the right thing are the same." She started to cry.

And:

The reason I finally got to see the baby that brought joy and happiness to my life was because her mom understood how I felt. She understood that it was sad for me to not be able to see her. She said that she felt it was time for me to be happy.

These narratives provide examples of young readers and writers applying lessons from literature to their own narrated memories. They wrote stories of when they or another narrator (or character) came to be more empathetic for another and consequently positively influenced both the writer and others in the story. They applied empathetic lessons from the literature to their own life stories.

Knoeller also discusses the importance of narrative when responding to literary texts when he writes, "narrative is especially well suited to considering a story from alternative perspectives" (2003, p. 46), such as when retelling a story from the point of view of another character. The studies in Ms. Madison's class did more than retell; they wrote their own narratives reflecting a similar theme—learning to empathize with others. I argue this may be even more powerful than retelling, as the young writers had to understand the story and respond to it by applying its message to their own experience, in an original narrative.

While it was often difficult for the teachers at College Town Middle School to find time to add literary texts, particularly long ones, they did find a way to introduce new, short narratives into their curriculum and guide students to respond empathetically, even within the standards-driven curriculum. However, we wonder how much deeper student response might have been if even more literature had been included, including full-length novels, and if additional class time were spent on discussion and written response. We feel we only scratched the surface of what was possible.

"They can do the worksheets; they're trained to do those": *Teacher exit interviews*

One last piece of interesting data from the study comes in the form of the transcribed teacher exit interviews which we conducted at the end of the study about their experience of teaching for social imagination or theory of mind. We transcribed and coded these interviews, and identified the following conceptual themes which shed some light on the study's results, and help us understand the challenges, and possible benefits, of teaching literature for increased social understanding in the middle school.

One theory is that the teachers, who cared very much about literary study, simply did not have the time and space in an increasingly standardized curriculum to integrate literature to the extent that would be necessary for young readers to experience narrative worlds and the resultant benefits. It's also important to note that the four teachers in the case study were working with the CCSS, which, as discussed in previous chapters, tend to be New Critical and behavioristic in their approach to literature, valuing outcomes that can be quantified. As we've seen, such approaches are rarely conducive to literature pedagogies that value readers identifying and empathizing with characters, thinking critically but not narrowly about themes and issues, and engaging in social action as a result of narrative experience.

In the following descriptions of the themes and issues that arose from the interviews, we share the teachers' thoughts about this quandary as well as other challenges they faced teaching literature to adolescents at College Town Middle School.

"One of the things we really tried to do with this research project . . . was to give it a connection to what we were also doing in the classroom": The failure of a square peg in a round hole

The first theme arising from the qualitative analysis of the interviews we have labeled "a square peg in a round hole," shows that the teachers' responses reflect an overall sense of frustration about integrating the new narrative texts chosen for the study into their existing curriculum. Just as the students would get settled into research responsibilities, for example, it would be time for another seemingly disconnected literature empathy activity. Students ultimately resisted. The teachers were trying to weave the collaboratively created assignments into their curricula while continuing to focus on teaching the state-mandated standards and preparing students for the state's standardized test. Even though they had volunteered to be a part of the study, they sometimes became frustrated. They couldn't get into the computer lab for a planned literature activity. The students seemed shocked by the sudden change in emphasis (What's all this about connecting with characters, anyway?). Teachers were sometimes bothered that these activities seemed like square pegs in round holes. With the state exam and the research project happening in the same semester, the teachers wrestled with schedules, and it was often difficult for them to even include the activities in our study. According to Mr. House, a teacher in the study:

> It seemed like this year we struggled to maybe put things in a certain order. To get it to work out with ISTEP [Indiana Statewide Testing for Educational Progress], our twenty-day ISTEP prep calendars. It seems like we're being asked to do a lot more. I mean if we did that, if we did these activities [from the empathy research] more in the first nine weeks, it would be a little bit better. So far from ISTEP, you can do a little bit more. It's easier to do things in the fall rather than the spring.

Mr. Sommers, quoted in the subheading and another teacher with whom we worked, suggested that it was not the order of events that disrupted his schedule and disconnected his students; it was, quite simply, our study itself. If, as he proposed, he had been given the time to connect the empathy activities to an existing unit plan, the chances of students having more, and deeper, empathic connections would have increased. In his reflection on the study's events, he concluded:

> If this [study] was something we were going to do and look at, I would make sure it was a part of an overall thematic unit. Something we don't feel like we're trying to squeeze into something else that we're doing.

Overall, due to what was perhaps poor researcher planning, coupled with tightly structured curricular scheduling tied to testing deadlines and requirements, the teachers never felt as if the literature activities developed for the study were adequately, much less seamlessly, integrated into their lessons and units. If the teachers thought these activities were square pegs in round holes, what must the students have thought?

"I think that they enjoyed . . . those kind of activities as opposed to a worksheet where they are having to answer comprehension questions": The reliance on fill-in-the-blank

The second theme emerging from the interviews was an overall sense that students were more comfortable with traditional, fill-in-the-blank worksheets than with other types of literary response, such as writing, discussion, or group activities, even if the active or creative responses might ultimately be more interesting to them, as Ms. Madison's comment in the subheading suggests. Honestly, what we discovered throughout the study was that what we were asking the teachers (and in turn, the students) to do created a fair amount of classroom discomfort.

When we approached the College Town teachers about this empathy research project, they seemed well on board. We had animated conversations about the project, our expectations, the use of YA novels and the importance of adolescents stepping into a character's shoes and experiences. But even with these well-intentioned attempts to allow students to be creative, the first assignment was a poem written in a structured line-by-line format that the students had done earlier in the year for another assignment: the "I am" poem mentioned earlier in this chapter. Despite the impressive responses of the so-called "big movers" discussed earlier, Ms. Madison described the "I am" poem as, "literally 'I am,' and then it gives in parenthesis how you're supposed to fill in those blanks. It's open ended in that you get to choose, but it's very structured." It could be said that the response poem was itself a type of worksheet.

Worksheets are familiar and repetitive. When curriculum mandates projects and canonical material by grade level that must be accomplished every year, there is less and less room for teacher—or student—creativity and ingenuity. Mr. Sommers suggested that this first activity, while still highly structured, offered the students a non-traditional spin on the worksheet, as it was "[A] lot better than a traditional worksheet, where we feed that information to them instead of [them] discovering that on their own." He went on to say, "[Students] can do worksheets. They're trained to do those.... They see a worksheet format and they go into worksheet mode. We've trained them pretty well on how we want them to complete those assignments." We would agree that students are well trained on worksheets and, overall, find them comfortable and comforting. It's perhaps no surprise that the students making the highest gains on the empathy scale were those who were immersed most deeply in creative, imaginative responses, responses that went past knee-jerk blank filling.

Overall, the teachers seemed well aware that their students were more comfortable filling out worksheets than engaging in creative, imaginative or reflective assignments in response to literature. When they attempted to open the door to creativity and emotional response, while it was sometimes successful, in general intellectual, emotional and behavioral disconnect were the result.

"Perhaps, I was a little more into our research paper. We did [the study's] assignment as a break. But my mind was on [the research paper]. The kids' minds were on that": The curricular disconnect

The last theme we identified we have named "curricular disconnect," as it refers to a feeling among the teachers that the new texts and activities did not relate to other big assignments such as the research project, and therefore often felt unrelated to required class lessons or activities. According to the participants, each teacher had trouble finding space in an already jam-packed schedule to include texts that were not supported by the scheduled curriculum. In fact, the teachers claimed they barely had time to squeeze in the final empathy activity, which resulted in another disjointed attempt to encourage creativity that did not seem to fit with the surrounding days and weeks of school. Ms. Madison said:

> That [final] lesson wasn't as successful, I feel, as the first one. I think they needed more time to do it. We just did it in one class period. The stories. And it just wasn't as, I wasn't as happy with that one as I was the first one. It didn't mesh as well as I had hoped.

The teachers also scrutinized whether it was the texts' disconnect from their classroom plans that led to student disengagement and apparent apathy. Mr. Sommers suggested that the first story, Gary Soto's "Born Worker" was successful because the students were already working with narrative text and creative writing and a poetic response seemed more natural. However, once the class plan steered toward the research project, the students seemed to disconnect from subsequent empathy-building activities, as his quote in the subheading reflects. During the Holocaust story activity, Mr. Sommers stated:

> I think they developed a better understanding of the characters in the "Born Worker" story especially. Because that was one of the goals of the poem [to understand character]. They were able to look at it [the story], and I had them look at it from different perspectives. And I think that helps them with character development. . . . With the Holocaust story, I don't think they connected to that story as well. They connected to the idea of the Holocaust in part because they had their own knowledge of it with what they were reading and studying. [However] I don't think it directly related to the assignment they did.

Essentially, the activity and first story were included in a thematic unit that somewhat valued the study's personal, creative connections. The final activity and text, however, did not so much. Shoved into a research unit, the Holocaust text and subsequent assignment were missing the personal, creative connections and instead activated students' prior objective knowledge. What is interesting here is that the teachers agree, on many levels, that the disconnection experienced by the students was due to their inability, or unwillingness, to learn or experience diverse classroom content simultaneously. As suggested, a poem and a short story, although squeezed together, fit well enough; a research project and a short story seem at odds, as the teachers made clear in their exit interviews.

"It's like, did I really reach them? Was I really able to change their mind, their thinking, their mind frame about something?" What we learned about narrative experiences of teens

Ms. Madison asked the question in this subheading, and it's a valid one. Much of the research cited in this book tells us that literature can change the minds of readers, can shift perspectives and even unravel biases. However, what we learned from this case study was that there must be curricular and institutional supports in place for this change to happen; teaching literature to enrich theory of mind, or deepen understandings of diverse people, places, and events, doesn't happen unless such experience is prioritized in schools and is provided with appropriate time and resources. However, time and resources in education tend to follow the priorities of our policy-makers, who are currently concerned with quantifying and comparing schools and teachers in the service of accountability and over-simplified, sometimes flawed, notions of global competition.

To specifically shine the light on adolescents' empathic relationships with fictional texts, we learned that forcing such activities and instruction into an already constructed curriculum isn't the best plan. It wasn't that students were not capable of empathetic responses to fiction, or that teachers didn't value such responses. Instead we learned that standardized exams and curricula designed to match them sometimes do not allow teachers to focus on personal, or emotional, response, even when the argument could be made that such responses are connected to critical cognition. There are too many skills and competencies to be mastered; thus, there was just not time to encourage personal student connections with texts.

Our critique here is not to be confused with an indictment of teacher practice at College Town. More so, this is a reflection and critique of educational expectations and an assessment-driven curriculum (as well as perhaps a critique of our own process as researchers). We believe the four teachers in this study did a wonderful job teaching their students language arts and literature within the bureaucratized educational climate in which they, and many other teachers in the US, currently work. With additional time and autonomy we think their influence could be far greater.

Note: We thank all the teachers and students who participated in this project.

References

Jolliffe, D. & Farrington, D.P. (2006). Development and validation of the basic empathy scale. *Journal of Adolescence*, 29, 589–611.

Knoeller, C. (2003). Imaginative response: Teaching literature through creative writing. *The English Journal*, 92(5), 42–48.

Lowry, Lois (1993). *The Giver*. New York: Houghton Mifflin.

Miller, S.J., Burns, L.D. & Johnson, T.S. (2013). *Generation Bullied 2.0: Prevention and intervention strategies for our most vulnerable students*. Bern, Switzerland: Peter Lang.

Indiana Department of Education (2011). A–F Accountability. November. Retrieved from www.doe.in.gov/accountability/f-accountability

Soto, G. (2006). *Petty crimes*. New York: HMH Books for Young Readers.

Wisenberg, S.L. (2002). *Holocaust girls: History, memory, and other obsessions*. Lincoln, Nebraska: Bison Books.

PART III

Reviving the Secondary School Literary Experience

The potential implications for secondary English teaching of the loss of literary study are great. Both teachers and teacher educators might begin to think about how they can retain literature in their classrooms, programs, and schools. Teaching literature for profit would be a dramatic paradigm shift, a shift that many English teachers and teacher educators (and very possibly others) would regret. Literature may not make readers more moral, but it may move them in that direction—or, at least, provide the opportunity to think through moral conundrums.

Full Circle

When I was a sophomore in high school, I was assigned *To Kill a Mockingbird*, a "classic" I'd actually known little about up to that point. I began reading the assigned pages the same way I would've any assigned text, by speed-reading and highlighting sporadically. I noticed quickly, however, that *Mockingbird* wasn't like most school-chosen pieces of literature. With a protagonist I could relate to (Scout) and a topic I was genuinely interested in (civil rights), I began to dig into the lives of the citizens of Maycomb and the events that occurred there.

Up to that point, my reading repertoire had been full of murder mysteries and young adult fantasies—nothing like the historically-set fiction Harper Lee offered the world. (Which, in hindsight, makes it even more odd that I became attached to *Mockingbird* at all!)

Regardless, this book stuck with me long after I graduated high school. It was one of the few books I took with me to college, and one that I read over again every year or so. While in college, I went through a period of not knowing what I wanted to do with my life. I'd switched concentrations once or twice, when I finally realized it'd been staring me in the face for years now. I loved to read and I enjoyed working with people, so, putting those together, I decided to become a high school English teacher—the same person that introduced me to *Mockingbird*!

My relationship with *Mockingbird* came full circle when, during my student teaching experience, I was asked to teach the very piece of fiction I'd carried with me since high school. Needless to say, my creativity went wild and my students found themselves right in the middle of Maycomb County, experiencing fiction in the classroom like never before.

By James Herman

Creating Readers

During my third year of teaching I was charged with a small, eclectic group of below grade-level, reluctant readers in my sixth hour class. It was as if I'd walked into the film *The Breakfast Club*: the jock, the troublemaker, the princess, the tomboy, and the class clown. All misunderstood—all hating my subject, expressed by looks of disdain only angsty teenagers have mastered. The year drudged on, and I tried every activity, every type of material, and every method of motivation I could muster. Still, by winter break, I felt I was getting nowhere. With the ECA (end of course assessment) right around the corner, these students were still refusing to read, and were therefore not acquiring the skills they so needed to acquire.

When we came back from some much-needed and refreshing time off, I decided to try something I hadn't before: *Divergent* by Veronica Roth. At first, the students were put off by the sheer size of the book. I was met with not-so-subtle displeasure, and the students were very blunt in their insistence that they would not, under any circumstances read this book. Fine, I told them. And I began reading it to them.

By the time we finished the first chapter, they were hooked. They asked questions about the dystopian society, how it came to be, and why the characters lived the way they did. They were especially concerned with the fact that the 16-year-old protagonist was forced to choose who she was at such a ripe age, when they, at the same age, didn't know who they were. As we delved deeper into the novel, I saw a change in the students. They begged to spend class time reading, and not so they could get out of written work—so that they could actually *read*. Their written responses became engaging and thought provoking. Their discussions became meaningful. The day we finished the novel, they begged me to get the sequel, *Insurgent*, for them. Who was I to deprive thirsty readers of that which they craved?

At the end of the year, we found out that all five of the students had passed the ECA, including the one who had told me on the first day, "I'm not passing that test because I'm not smart enough." I don't take credit; I credit the literature that sucked them into a world to which they had previously been hesitant to enter. Each of those students are now successful in their subsequent English classes, and make a point to stop into my room to tell me what new, exciting book they are reading. It's every teacher's dream, and I was fortunate enough to experience it.

By Paige Clinkenbeard

References

Roth, V. (2011). *Divergent*. New York: Katherine Tegen Books.
Roth, V. (2012). *Insurgent*. New York: Katherine Tegen Books.

8

IMPLICATIONS FOR ENGLISH
TEACHER EDUCATION

> We urge English educators to consider the importance of the type of indoctrination that students get in a preservice program. If the program teaches them the importance of understanding the source of a knowledge base through an understanding of the people behind it, then we see the likelihood that they will see research as being conducted by people with beliefs and agendas and not simply accept (or, on the contrary, distrust) everything that comes their way preceded by "Research says . . . ."
>
> *(Smagorinsky & Whiting, 1995, p. 110)*

I have argued for the continued teaching of literature in the secondary school by looking at policy and politics, research in various related and relevant disciplines and settings, and historical overviews of literature curriculum in the 20th and 21st centuries. Before concluding with some summary thoughts, I take time here to relate these arguments to the English education methods classroom, a classroom in which I spend a great deal of my own professional time.

Literature teaching is a staple in many English education methods or pedagogy courses, and I have no reason to believe it won't continue to be. However, the way literature is taught in middle and high schools has changed as standards-based initiatives, such as the Common Core State Standards and other similar sets of standards, which respond to our nation's obsession with quantitative measures and business-like accountability, proliferate. Sometimes "reading" or "literature" classes are split from so-called "English" or "language" classes, isolating literary study from other rhetorical aspects of the English language arts, and sometimes replacing literature study altogether with nonfiction reading and/or independent reading of grade-leveled books. In contrast, literature methods courses (or general methods courses that incorporate literature teaching) seem to have changed little in the last fifteen to twenty years. We still tend to value response-based pedagogies, cultural studies approaches, and thematic planning, as described in Chapter 6.

While the politics of literature teaching, and teaching in general, are sometimes a part of literature methods classes, particularly when philosophies for why literature should be taught are mentioned, it seems that teacher candidates are mostly advised to reject the standardized, mechanical and rote approaches reflected in standards-based curriculum and standardized testing and instead follow the student-centered approaches that are consistent with many of the approaches suggested in this book—teaching literature for personal, as well as cognitive-intellectual, growth. However, this position can put teacher candidates in a bind, as they are at once taught literature pedagogies in college that value narrative fiction for its personal, transformative powers, while simultaneously transitioning into a professional role that asks, or even compels, them to teach in a sometimes strikingly different way. How to deal with such contradictions professionally and efficiently may very well be a skill we are not teaching them. In fact, we often pretend that the contradiction doesn't even exist, since it may not have when we were high school English teachers years ago.

So what does all this mean for the instructor of college-level English education courses that prepare new teachers to teach in this environment? In what follows, I begin by offering my reflections on how literature methods courses have been traditionally structured, primarily by using my own teaching as an example. Then, I deconstruct this traditional structure to offer new ways of thinking about preparing new teachers to teach literature, ways that are attuned to the challenges of teaching literature in an age of standardization and scientific objectivity. Next, I summarize what might happen to the profession and, by association, secondary schools if literary study continues to find itself under the gun and current decreases in enrollments in teacher education programs continue. Finally, I summarize professional resources that might assist in the process.

The Philosophy on Which the Course is Based

In my syllabus for a methods course about how to teach literature to adolescents (which I have taught at my university numerous times) I wrote, in part:

> This course will explore several aspects of teaching literature in high schools in an effort to prepare you for the job of creating and nurturing young readers: These facets include 1) reasons for including literature in the curriculum and how to select literature for classroom use; 2) suggestions for devising and implementing a response-based literature program; 3) approaches to teaching young adult literature; 4) strategies for assisting struggling readers, and 5) exploration of professional resources concerning the teaching of literature in the secondary school.
>
> *(See the entire syllabus at: http://web.ics.purdue.edu/~alsupj/492.htm)*

This description of the course and its aims and purposes is relatively straightforward and pragmatic in tone and content. I write about how to select literature, how to create curriculum, and how to devise daily lessons that meet the needs of diverse students. All of these things are important for sure, and there's nothing incorrect about emphasizing them in a syllabus for a course called "teaching literature in the secondary school." However, it leaves out much of what has been revealed in this book, as it assumes that everyone is on board with the teaching of literature in the first place, that the emphasis should always be on student responses to literature, and that teachers will and should have autonomy over book selection and lesson planning. However, it seems that these assumptions might be held only by English teachers and English teacher educators, not by policy-makers, many lay citizens, and some school administrators. I remember that when I started teaching I was advised by colleagues to just close my door and teach—forget about the politics and policies and do my own thing. I don't know if that was good advice then, and I think it may be even worse advice now—in fact, perhaps impossible, or destructive advice for a new teacher in today's educational climate. Putting one's head in the sand seems no longer a viable option.

So what advice do I have for revising my own course description? I would perhaps keep the practical advice, but add the political dimension to it—complicate the picture, so to speak. Yes, teachers should be able to choose their own books based on their professional knowledge and education, but what to do if that isn't the case? Yes, we believe that it is important to teach full-length novels and short fiction in an English class in middle or high school, but if the curriculum doesn't allow room, what is the compromise? And, yes, while response-based curricula might be our approach of choice, when more restrictive, standards-based curriculum is required, how do you make sure that strategies encouraging empathy or identification aren't truncated or dismissed entirely? In short, the reality of today's secondary school literature class is more complex than the language of my syllabus implies.

Course Texts

In my syllabus, I identified and required the following course texts (note: I taught this course in 2002):

- *Literature and Lives: A Response-Based, Cultural Studies Approach to Teaching English* (2001) by Allen Carey-Webb
- *Critical Encounters in High School English: Teaching Literary Theory to Adolescents* (2000/2009) by Deborah Appleman
- *From Hinton to Hamlet: Building Bridges Between Young Adult Literature and the Classics* (1996/2005) by Sarah K. Herz with Donald Gallo

As I look at these book selections, I still like them. However, I would not make the same selections today. As noted in Chapter 6 about curriculum, I might select texts that reflect a "literacy practices approach" such as Beach et al.'s *Teaching to Exceed the English Language Arts Common Core State Standards: A Literacy Practices Approach for 6–12 Classrooms* (2012), which not only sees literature as part of a larger instructional picture, one that includes real-world application and relevance, but also recognizes and confronts standardization not by shutting the door and carrying on as normal, but by evaluating its effects and making improvements within the required, bureaucratic structure. We want new teachers to make positive change, but they can only do that by keeping their jobs. In short, course texts should balance English Language Arts (ELA) theory and practice, as presented in the texts I chose above, with contemporary readings from theorists, researchers and even journalists that exemplify and elucidate the cultural battle currently underway between scientific objectivity and humanistic knowledge.

Course Requirements

I identified eight course assignments on my syllabus in 2002. These included an in-class partner literature teaching experience, a presentation about online literature teaching resources, a project connecting a YA and a "classic" text in a unit plan, and a "photographic philosophies" project for which students take photos representing their literature teaching philosophies. Upon reflection, these course assignments have many positive characteristics. They are varied, require individual and group work, demand efficient research in various environments, ask students to communicate orally and in writing, and require students to plan and deliver literature lessons. The photographic philosophies assignment even asks them to think about their developing professional identities. Also, in retrospect, these assignments seem consistent with the argument of this book which is, in part, that teachers should think about the importance of literary teaching in ways that embrace what literature itself can do for individual readers, in addition to the transferable skills reading fiction can impart to help students with other intellectual tasks. However, thinking about revision as I reach the end of this book, I would suggest to my former self that I ask students to think harder about how the encouragement of identification, empathy, critical thinking and social action might be integrated into their lessons and how these concepts might be more specifically linked to various literary texts and pedagogical techniques or strategies the teacher candidates consider for their future adolescent students. I would also encourage myself to not only ask students to use the Internet to research young adult authors or lesson ideas, but to think about how online and web 2.0 environments have changed the very nature of how adolescents read. As I mention in the Introduction, it is easy to see technology in competition with humanistic study such as the reading of literature, but perhaps a more welcoming position toward technology could have been reflected in my course syllabus: technology not only as a way to learn *about* literature, but as a type of literature itself.

Smagorinsky and Whiting, in *How English Teachers Get Taught: Methods of Teaching The Methods Class* (1995), examined eighty-one English education methods syllabi and discovered that transactional theories of literary response were commonly included, although emphasized variably (p. 71). I think that's true of my syllabus, which certainly values response-based, transactional approaches; however, there are many other assumptions about why, how, and when literature should and could be taught to adolescents. I would encourage my former (and current) self to interrogate these assumptions both on the syllabus and in class; students deserve to understand the challenges that await them and not to be lulled into thinking the teaching of literary fiction as presented by many university professors is universally uncontested and valued.

What Professional Organizations Say

Another resource for English teacher educators is professional organizations. While I have alluded to National Council of Teachers of English (NCTE) position statements and resolutions earlier in this book when discussing scripted curricula, I'd like to mention two here directly related to my argument for the continued teaching of literature in secondary school.

First, is the 2006 position statement, "Resolution on the Essential Roles and Value of Literature in the Curriculum" (www.ncte.org/positions/statements/valueofliterature). The statement reads, in part:

> The current era of high-stakes testing has resulted in a narrowed curriculum in many schools, leaving little time or resources for extended interaction with literature. The Reading First Initiative of the No Child Left Behind Act of 2002 encourages the use of specific commercial reading programs, many of which make minimal use of authentic books.

After this recognition of the political forces working against literature instruction, the statement recommends that:

- reading curricula focus on selecting, reading, responding to, and analyzing a wide range of literature;
- a wide range of high-quality literature representing diverse experiences and perspectives be integrated into all content areas, including reading instruction;
- students engage in deep and extended experiences with full authentic texts rather than with adaptations; and
- students are guaranteed opportunities to select literature representing a variety of topics and degrees of difficulty.

It is clear that many of the challenges of today's political and cultural milieu have not cropped up overnight; they have been present in somewhat different forms for quite a while, and this statement remains eminently relevant.

Second is the just recently released NCTE guideline entitled, "Leisure Reading" (www.ncte.org/positions/statements/leisure-reading), which states in part:

> Research shows that leisure reading enhances students' reading comprehension, vocabulary development, general knowledge, and empathy for others, as well as their self-confidence as readers, motivation to read throughout their lives, and positive attitude toward reading.

This statement might have been created in response to the Common Core State Standards, which do not mention the importance of free reading or developing lifelong readers. It might also have been written in response to popular reports that teenagers no longer read for pleasure (see "Children, Teens, and Reading," 2014 for one example). Regardless, while it might seem startling that such a position needs to be taken at all (for this assumes that someone is in opposition), there it is in black and white. A position that it seemed necessary to take and important to publicize. Such position statements and resolutions are crucial for English educators to share with their teacher education candidates. New teachers should know that these things are up for debate.

The Threat of Decreasing Enrollments and Teacher Shortages

Another implication for English teacher education, a particularly dreary one, is the continuing decrease in the number of students choosing to be secondary school English teachers. At my university, the number of teacher candidates in our English education program has decreased by nearly 40 percent since 2005. The same or similar is true for our other undergraduate, non-teaching majors. While this decrease may not be a direct result of the political and cultural attacks on literary study described here, I believe it is part of the picture. It is now almost a commonplace that teachers in the US are the favorite scapegoats for all educational ills, and are at the center (of the target, that is) of most talk about reform and accountability. Many states, including California, Wisconsin, Florida, and Indiana among others have eliminated or weakened teachers' unions and/or teachers' rights to due process in the workplace, along with sometimes eliminating tenure and simultaneously decreasing funding for public education. One might ask, in this type of climate, what bright, young student would choose to become a teacher? What parent would support such a choice? The dropping numbers in English teacher education are not surprising given current attitudes and policies, particularly when coupled with the changing status of humanities and liberal arts programs I described in the Introduction. If the numbers continue to drop, teacher shortages seem likely, even though current projections in English language arts vary greatly state by state, and currently English teacher shortages are not projected for Indiana in the near future (Teacher Shortage Areas Nationwide Listing, 2014).

Despite published predictions, my university and others in our state have experienced sharp drops in numbers of students choosing to major in teaching since the early 2000s (Livingston, 2012). At the same time these drops are occurring among traditional teacher education programs, "fast track" or alternative teacher licensure programs are proliferating around the country, as every state has reported that it has some type of non-traditional route to teaching (NEA, 2014), even though they may vary in their course, credit hour and field experience requirements. Research has shown that the quality of alternative teacher education programs is variable, as there is little continuity or quality control (Editorial Projects in Education Research Center, 2004). An overview of existing research conducted by the Center for Urban and Multicultural Education at Indiana University (2006) concluded the following based on studies of alternative licensure programs conducted between 2000 and 2009:

> As a group, the studies find that teachers who are fully certified (through traditional college/university based teacher education programs) have a more significant positive impact on student outcomes than teachers who are not. . . . However, the substantial variation in requirements among AC programs raises questions about standards and minimum requirements, and more importantly, the impact on low income urban and rural minority populations when a significant portion of their teachers are not fully certified and/or have the appropriate skills and training to teach all children.
>
> *(p. 3)*

Linda Darling-Hammond's (2002) research on the results of teachers prepared through Teach for America demonstrated that TFA teachers perform about as well as other, traditionally prepared teachers but nearly all leave teaching in three years. Regardless of these perhaps non-alarming results, she goes on to warn that some, poorly done alternative routes to teaching *can* have negative effects on student learning. Also, it may not be in a school's best interest to have a new cadre of teachers every three years so that no teacher makes a long-term professional commitment, and the culture of the school is periodically disrupted. So again, the results are mixed, and I would argue that a revolving door approach to teaching is not the kind of professionalization we need to encourage.

Regardless, this proliferation of alternative, quicker and perhaps perceived as "easier" routes to becoming a licensed teacher may also be affecting undergraduate teacher enrollments in teacher education programs in my state and others, particularly as attitudes toward teachers continue to degrade, and in the field of English, opinions about the humanities continue to trend toward irrelevancy. In English teacher education this combination of the martyrdom of teachers, the increase in alternative teacher licensure routes, and the increasingly dismissive view of English studies as irrelevant to 21st century life, may be a death knell. But

I believe there is still hope on the horizon if English teachers and English teacher educators can make an argument for the future of literary studies in an era of vocationalization.

How Can English Teacher Educators Help Literature Remain in the Curriculum?

In closing, I believe this argument for teaching literature has great implications for teacher educators, the methods courses they (we) teach, and their teacher education students who will soon have their own ELA classrooms. English educators can raise student teacher awareness of the issues at stake and what might be lost if convincing arguments are not made in response to increasing standardization and top-down control of curriculum and text selection. It is no longer adequate to answer the question, "why do we teach literature, anyway?" with "it teaches critical thinking" or "it makes students kinder to others." While these statements might contain kernels of truth, there is a great deal more experiential and research evidence to support, enrich, and elucidate these oft-repeated and commonly rebuffed claims. English teachers and their students, as well as practicing secondary teachers, would benefit from being knowledgeable and conversant about this evidence.

References

Appleman, D. (2000/2009). *Critical encounters in high school English: Teaching literary theory to adolescents*. New York: Teachers College Press.

Beach, R., Thein, A.H. & Webb, A. (2012). *Teaching to exceed the English language arts common core state standards: A literacy practices approach for 6–12 classrooms*. New York: Routledge.

Center for Urban and Multicultural Education Indiana University School of Education (2006). *Teacher licensure (certification) research brief*. Retrieved August 28, 2014 from http://education.iupui.edu/CUME/

"Children, teens, and reading: a common sense research brief." (2014). San Francisco, CA: Common Sense Media. Retrieved December 31, 2014 from www.commonsensemedia. org/research/children-teens-and-reading

Darling-Hammond, L. (2002). Research and rhetoric on teacher certification: A response to teacher certification reconsidered. *Education Policy Analysis Archives*, 10(36).

Editorial Projects in Education Research Center. (2004). Issues A–Z: Alternative Teacher Certification. *Education Week*, August 3. Retrieved August 28, 2014 from www. edweek.org/ew/issues/alternative-teacher-certification/

Herz, S.K. & Gallo, D.R. (1996/2005). *From Hinton to Hamlet: Building bridges between young adult literature and the classics*. Westport, CT: Greenwood.

Livingston, M. (2012). Indiana education colleges see drop in enrollment, applications. *Journal and Courier* online. Retrieved August 28, 2014 from www.jconline.com/ article/20121127/NEWS04/112040001/Indiana-education-colleges-see-drop-enrollment-applications

NEA (2014). *Research spotlight on alternative routes to teacher certification: NEA reviews of the research on best practices in education*. National Education Association. Retrieved August 28, 2014 from www.nea.org/tools/16578.htm

Smagorinsky, P. & Whiting, M.E. (1995). *How English teachers get taught: Methods of teaching the methods class*. Urbana, IL: CEE and NCTE.

Teacher Shortage Areas Nationwide Listing: 1990–1991 through 2014–2015 (2014). Washington, DC: US Department of Education.

Webb, A.C. (2001). *Literature and lives: A response-based, cultural studies approach to teaching English*. Urbana, IL: NCTE.

9

TEACHING LITERATURE
FOR PROFIT OR PLEASURE?

Despite the fact that *A Nation At Risk* has been largely discredited in the 30 years since its publication and the dire condition of American schools has been greatly exaggerated for the purposes of perpetuating a crisis mentality in education, the rhetoric of reform in the United States continues to hold up economic success as the sole purpose of a K–12 education.

(Tienken & Orlich, quoted in Endacott and Goering, 2014, p. 89)

In this book I have made an argument for the continued teaching of literature in the secondary school through more than the ordinary means; rather than simply focusing on how literature can make students better thinkers in other disciplines or prepare them for college or career, I used theory and research from multiple disciplines to argue for the importance of reading narrative fiction. In doing so, I've also felt it to be important to summarize some existing challenges to literature teaching in education and in our culture at large; in other words, to explain why it is important to make this argument at all, and why it is now necessary. In the Introduction I noted that my goal was to make an argument for the teaching of literature grounded in historical thought and reality, policy analysis, scholarly research, and anecdotal teacher knowledge. I hope I have done that.

The goal of this chapter will be to bring the last few threads of the argument together, add a few missing pieces, and leave you, the reader, with some ideas for further consideration. I begin with a piece that is essential here, and to which I have already alluded, the notion that the standardized literature curriculum can actually be, or currently is, a money-making endeavor for some of those working in education policy and publishing. While I am not an expert in these corporate maneuvers, I try here to provide a brief outline of who, and what, may be corrupting literature teaching for potential profit. I end with an outline of what

I see as key points and ideas for ongoing consideration, for continued thought, reflection, discussion, research, and writing. These are things still on my mind, perhaps even more so, at the end of this writing process.

Teaching Literature for Profit

Several articles have been written over the last few years detailing the extent to which a few people, and a few corporations, seem to be using their money (and resultant power) to control, and "reform," American public education (see Ravitch, (2014a); Giroux, 2011; Ohanian, 2013).

In May 2014, two research articles were published in the *American Economic Review* lauding the importance of "value added" assessment of teachers. These articles, co-written by three Harvard professors, Raj Chetty, John Friedman, and Jonah Rockoff, describe a quasi-experimental research project examining the extent to which so-called VA (value added) teacher assessment positively affected more than 2.5 million 3rd through 8th graders. The first article looked at standardized test scores of students from 1989–2009, controlling for variables such as student demographics and prior achievement, to isolate the effects of teacher VA measurement. The second article focused on how "high-VA" teachers have long-term effects on students, such as lifetime earnings and college attendance (Chetty et al., 2014b, p. 1). In a nutshell, they found and reported that yes, VA measurements of teachers do increase test scores and long-term positive outcomes. So they concluded that using student test scores to evaluate teachers is a good thing.

Reports of these articles made the *New York Times* and PBS (Public Broadcasting Service). Diane Ravitch (2014b) wrote about them in her blog (http://dianer avitch.net/2014/06/02/raj-chetty-vam-audrey-amrein-beardsley-and-me/), recounting an online conversation she had with first author Chetty about the veracity and integrity of his work and its possible negative effect on teachers, schools, and children. In their publications, the Harvard economists go on to argue that value-added measures of primary school teachers, which use assessments of students' growth over time as largely determined through standardized test scores, to promote, reward, or fire teachers, would allow administrators to get rid of bad teachers early and hence improve teaching and learning. In the 2012 *New York Times* article by Annie Lowrey, Professor Friedman is quoted as saying, "the message is to fire people sooner rather than later" (unpaged).

But they don't stop there. In the two-part research report, the researchers address how "high-VA" teachers improve test scores, and then move to how these teachers affect students' future money-making potential. The researchers begin with the claim that they had "established that value-added measures can help us identify which teachers have the greatest ability to raise students' test scores" (Chetty et al., 2014a, p. 2623) and then go on to assert that students assigned to such high-VA teachers "are more likely to attend college, earn higher salaries, and are less likely to have children as teenagers" (Chetty et al., 2014b, p. 2633). Based on their analysis of school and tax records they even make hiring suggestions, writing, "Replacing a teacher whose VA [value added] is in the bottom 5% with an average teacher would increase the present value of students' lifetime income by approximately $250,000 per classroom" (p. 1).

Who would think that's a bad thing? We all want our children to be successful and earn a good living. But those of us who have taught may have a hard time accepting this easy correlation; we know that the effect of a "good" teacher is more complex a tale than the numbers tell. All in all, the Chetty et al. formula seems a little too easy. Are our educational woes so easily fixed? Is good teaching so easily assessed? Can decisions about teacher mentorship, professional development, and promotion be so cleanly made? What about student and family poverty? Broken families? Hunger? Learning a second language? No problem, I guess, as long as teachers with high VA scores are teaching, kids will probably go to college, earn good money and even won't get pregnant as teenagers. It is important to note that teachers and teacher educators may not be the only ones skeptical of VA measures; in April 2014 the American Statistical Association (ASA) published a report recommending that VA measures always be used in conjunction with other assessments, as they "do not directly measure potential teacher contributions toward other student outcomes" (ASA, 2014, p. 2). Unfortunately, this report has not gotten as much press as the Chetty et al. study.

VA measures are one example of money telling the tale of education, of education being viewed as, above all, a pathway to a quantifiable outcome. While Chetty et al. is only one research study, it seems to reflect the direction in which policy-makers, and many US citizens, are moving to determine the quality of US public education—it's an input/output business-like procedure. Put students in good schools with good teachers; get quantifiable, predictable results out. Very clean, very simple. Teachers are just cogs in a well-oiled machine.

My second example of education for profit is bigger than one research study; it's a complex web of corporations, politicians, and business-minded philanthropists. Two of the most obvious examples of corporate and foundation influence on education policy and practice are the Pearson Corporation and the Bill and Melinda Gates Foundation, although others are at work as well, including the Walton Foundation and the Lumina Foundation, which has recently teamed up with Gallup to create and administer several polls and surveys about education in the US, including ones administered by universities such as my own, to determine what kind of higher education leads to the most productive, and rewarding, life and career.

Pearson may be the most insidious player in the game to make profit from education, as they own multiple publishers of educational materials, such as Adobe, Scott Foresman, Penguin, and Prentice Hall, as well as many of the tests that enable entrance or exit from educational programs and institutions, including the General Education Development exam (GED), many teacher licensure content and pedagogy tests, and, in collaboration with Stanford University, the new edTPA (teacher performance assessment), which at this time is being considered by my state, and others, as another mandatory teacher licensure test taken during student teaching (it will cost about $300 to take the test). Pearson was also a key supporter of the Common Core State Standards (CCSS), which states must adopt if they want access to federal money through President Obama's "Race to the Top", as they are one of the three biggest textbook publishers in the US today (Job, 2012) and in the business of aligning their textbooks with CCSS tests to make them more saleable to Common Core states. Additionally, Pearson is collaborating with the Gates Foundation to figure out how to align online K–12 curriculum to the Common Core State Standards, curriculum which could potentially be sold to states and schools, along with the ability to store student "data" so it can be accessed later to track student performance over time—never mind that many are concerned about what this data will include, and how and with whom it will be shared. It appears that Pearson has its hand in all levels of K–12 education, beginning with teacher education and ending with the assessment of the K–12 teachers themselves, who are increasingly evaluated by student test scores. Teacher education programs might also soon be drawn into the web if they are evaluated by the performance of their students' students, an approach favored by US Secretary of Education Arne Duncan.

Interestingly, just recently the Gates Foundation has called for a delay in evaluating teachers based on student scores on exams linked to the CCSS, so that teachers can become more prepared to teach the standards (Feeney, 2014). However, the Gates Foundation's connection to writing, and lobbying for, the CCSS is clear, as they have spent more than $200 million in grants and political lobbying supporting the standards during their development and implementation (Layton, 2014). One might wonder why the Gates Foundation is so interested in supporting the CCSS. It could be that Gates and his staff simply want to improve US education. However, it could also be, as Layton writes, "a fragmented education system stifled innovation because textbook publishers and software developers were catering to a large number of small markets instead of exploring breakthrough products" (unpaged). Perhaps Bill Gates saw some economic benefit to the consolidation of so many education markets.

There have always been standards and tests to test them, at least since I became a teacher in 1989. However, those developing, funding, and supporting these standards and related texts and tests seem to be qualitatively different than in the past. There are fewer on-the-ground educators involved and more corporate executives, testing companies (e.g., the College Board, ETS, ACT Inc.), and private foundations (e.g., Gates, Achieve) with a personal, financial stake in how our children are tested and taught. And, perhaps most disturbingly, many of these individuals, companies, think tanks, and foundations are connected through lobbying efforts, shared boards and committees, or even shared or shifting employees, as some individuals move from company to company as their status, and earning power, increases (e.g., Michael Barber's work in Tony Blair's administration as an education reformer, then at global consulting firm McKinsey and Company, and finally his current job as Chief Education Advisor at Pearson) (Zancanella & Moore, 2014, pp. 273–274). This web of corporate influence and control is difficult for anyone to sort out, especially given that the organizations themselves do not wish to be seen as collaborators in a common mission to make money on the backs of school children, teachers, and parents.

After viewing the connections and the collaborations, it's hard not to see the writing on the wall: US public education is being controlled, and "reformed," by a few powerful individuals with monetary agendas. Literature teaching and learning is, of course, included here, especially when thinking about initiatives such as text complexity bands and informational texts, as discussed earlier in this book. Literature isn't being treated any differently than any other subject area or testable collection of content—it is being oversimplified, quantified, and re-packaged for assessment and subsequent application to material goals, such as high employability and income, goals important to a possession-driven culture.

Teaching Literature for Pleasure

Of course, as the previous chapters have outlined, there are more reasons to teach literature than just because it is pleasurable to read. While enjoyment certainly has a place in school, there are other, many other, good reasons for reading, teaching and responding to literary texts, including increased understandings of self and others, increased motivation to engage in socially conscious actions, and deeper critical thinking merging the cognitive and the affective. However, I believe many of these results occur as a by-product of pleasure. Students who have never read a complete novel, never lost the sense of time and place while reading an engaging story, or never imagined themselves in a narrative world, are unlikely to experience the before-mentioned positive results of reading.

When schools, policy-makers, corporations, cultural myths, and policies decide and convey that literary studies, and by extension the humanities, are content-less, rigor-less, non-intellectual pastimes that can only be defended by their use in the service of other, more important, quantitative, objectively defined scientific disciplines and careers, then the literary experience begins to disappear in schools, as teachers, administrators and then students oust literature in favor of explicitly tested and externally valued knowledge. Young people stop reading. Teachers stop teaching novels and short stories longer than a few sentences. The lifelong reader no longer exists. Narrative experience is confined to Hollywood movies and video games—no one is any longer lost in a book.

While some may not think losing literary reading is a loss, I do. English teachers must continue to ask students to read and respond to narrative fictional texts. But is it too late? Has the fight already been lost? I don't think so. I think there are new teachers, and old ones, who daily determine to include literature, and by association the literary experience, in their secondary school classrooms, as the lesson plans and assignments included in this book testify. Despite all the roadblocks they persist, because they have experienced narrative worlds themselves, have seen students experience them, and they know personally and anecdotally what literature has done for themselves and others. I hope this book can add a little more substance to their fight, to their knowledge of the usefulness and power of literature for adolescents. I hope the information in this book can help them fight their fight better, stronger, and more efficiently.

So what are the takeaways? As I leave this text, I am left with the following questions, thoughts, and considerations as we continue to make a case for teaching literature in the secondary school, a case that admittedly includes as many subjective, as objective, reasons. You may have your own reasons to add, which I hope you will.

Reading changes readers

Reading fiction can change readers, as demonstrated through experience, intuition and empirical research. While there is still more to be learned about how, when and why these changes occur, it seems clear that they do. And the changes appear to be positive: deeper understandings of others, wider views of possibilities, and more tolerance and compassion toward difference. Many young people do not feel motivated or compelled to read, especially fiction, as they are distracted and even overwhelmed by jobs, school obligations, extra curriculars, shifting individual and group identities and mass media culture. Even though there are wide-ranging obstacles to teaching literature and encouraging literary reading in schools, it seems that the obstacles may be worth challenging given the possible payoff. I think every novel and short story I've read has changed me in some way, whether I can explicitly describe how or not. In short, after reading I think I understood my fellow humans a little better.

Readers can change society

If we accept the above point as true, how can these same readers not make positive changes in the world? Readers interact with others, and they can serve as models of empathy and understanding. While concrete links between reading and behavior change and are still in the making, and connections between literary reading and morality or ethics are even more difficult, or even dangerous, to assert, it appears logical that if empathy is heightened through reading (and empathy *is* linked empirically to prosocial behavior) that reading must be *a* way, *one* way, to encourage positive social action. Through actions, affected by subjectivities and dispositions influenced by literary experience, I argue that readers of fiction may act in the world differently, more generously, and hence change it for the better. This is not to say that non-readers make no difference; such a generalization would be absurd. However, the reader of fiction appears to gain extra insight and have added opportunity to explore ethical and personal dilemmas that can lead to real-world action.

All knowledge is dependent on creative and imaginative thought

The separation between branches of knowledge, such as humanities, sciences, technology, STEM, STEAM, etc., is not only obstructionist, divisive and an over-simplified understanding of all these disciplines, it undermines, even dissuades, young people from crossing over, from liking not just science *or* English but *both*, from seeing how knowledge in many disciplines interacts, overlaps, feeds and enriches the other. We are impeding the thinking and decision-making of young people by institutionalizing and encouraging the elevation of one discipline over another, rather than urging our youth to study widely, read often, and think creatively. But all is not lost. At my university, for example, attempts are being made to integrate liberal arts and sciences, and a new multi-disciplinary undergraduate program is in development. I hope this program will contain opportunities for literary reading. As reading fiction and imagination are inherently linked, such experience can only enrich other knowledge.

Human connections further humanity

Today we need young people who will be thoughtful, caring, understanding, yet open to considering the point of view of others. We need young people who think, read, ask questions, travel, imagine, and connect knowledge from various forms and sources and contexts. At a time of school shootings so common that they seem normal (as I write this on June 12, 2014, CNN is reporting there have been 74 school shootings since the Sandy Hook massacre in December 2012), when bullying is so rampant that the word itself is becoming a cliché, when leaders can't compromise on any issue however small, we need education that opens rather than closes and policies that don't serve as a means to punish teachers and schools or situate parents and teachers as enemies rather than allies. We need policies that aren't obsessed with comparisons between teachers, schools, states or countries but that are instead concerned with helping students learn and think and feel and imagine. Roxana Robinson wrote in a recent *New York Times* opinion piece that writers of stories must always be prepared for "radical empathy" (2014, p. 8) to influence their creations. I think readers should be prepared as well.

I'm not sure how we can accomplish all of the positive changes in the world we might desire, but I do feel that teaching literature, asking adolescents to read and respond to narrative fiction, may help. Without literature, without the literary experience, we continue to dehumanize the humanities, segregate and sanitize disciplines, and turn school into a means to an end rather than a holistic preparation for life, a goal not assessable through a standardized test and not affected by ever-changing standards or large corporations writing and selling tests.

I'm not claiming teaching and reading literature will solve all our problems, but I am suggesting it's a start. Furthermore, it's a plan that English teachers, students and teacher educators can support, even champion.

After all, we know that reading fiction matters.

References

ASA (2014). Statement on using value-added models for educational assessment. American Statistical Association, April 8. Retrieved from www.washingtonpost.com/blogs/answer-sheet/wp/2014/04/13/statisticians-slam-popular-teacher-evaluation-method/

Chetty, R., Friedman, J.N. & Rockoff, J.E. (2014a). Measuring the impacts of teachers I: Evaluating bias in teacher value-added estimates. *American Economic Review*, 104(9): 2593–2632.

Chetty, R., Friedman, J.N. & Rockoff, J.E. (2014b). Measuring the impacts of teachers II: Teacher value-added and student outcomes in adulthood. *American Economic Review*, 104(9): 2633–2679.

Endacott, J.L. & Goering, C.Z. (2014). Speaking truth to power: Reclaiming the conversation on education. *English Journal*, 103(5), 89–92.

Feeney, N. (2014). Gates Foundation calls for delay in "common core"-based teacher evaluations. *Time*, June 10, 2014. Retrieved from http://time.com/2854644/gates-foundation-common-core-delay/

Giroux, H.A. (2011). *Education and the crisis of public values: Challenging the assault on teachers, students, and public education*. New York: Peter Lang.

Job, J. (2012). The Pearson monopoly. *Newteacher*. Retrieved from http://teacherblog.typepad.com/newteacher/2012/11/on-the-rise-of-pearson-oh-and-following-the-money.html

Layton, L. (2014). How Bill Gates pulled off the swift common core revolution. *The Washington Post*, June 7. Retrieved from www.washingtonpost.com/politics/how-bill-gates-pulled-off-the-swift-common-core-revolution/2014/06/07/a830e32e-ec34-11e3-9f5c-9075d5508f0a_story.html

Lowrey, A. (2012). Big study links good teachers to lasting gain. *New York Times*, January 6, 2012. Retrieved from www.nytimes.com/2012/01/06/education/big-study-links-good-teachers-to-lasting-gain.html?pagewanted=all&_r=0

Ohanian, S. (2013). Whoo-hoo! Occupy the schools. *Daily Censored*, February 19. Retrieved from www.dailycensored.com/woo-hoo/

Ravitch, D. (2014a). *Reign of error: The hoax of the privatization movement and the danger to America's public schools*. New York: Alfred Knopf.

Ravitch, D. (2014b). Raj Chetty, VAM, Audrey Amrein-Beardsley, and Me. Retrieved from http://dianeravitch.net/2014/06/02/raj-chetty-vam-audrey-amrein-beardsley-and-me/

Robinson, R. (2014). The Right to Write. *The New York Times*, June 29, 2014. Retrieved from http://opinionator.blogs.nytimes.com/2014/06/28/the-right-to-write/?_php=true&_type=blogs&_r=0/

Zancanella, D. & Moore, M. (2014). The origins of the common core: Untold stories. *Language Arts*, 91(4), 273–279.

10

LITERATURE AND MORALITY

It [the fairy story] is accused of giving children a false impression of the world they live in. But I think no literature that children could read gives them less of a false impression. I think what profess to be realistic stories for children are far more likely to deceive them. I never expected the real world to be like the fairy tales. I think that I did expect school to be like the school stories. The fantasies did not deceive me: the school stories did. All stories in which children have adventures and successes which are possible, in the sense that they do not break the laws of nature, but almost infinitely improbable, are in more danger than the fairy tales of raising false expectations.

(Lewis, C. S., 1952, p. 4)

A couple of weeks ago I was in my home state of Missouri, visiting my alma mater and my mother. In the city of Columbia, there is a small, funky bookshop called The Peace Nook. Whenever I return I make a point of going in to browse, as I can learn as much, as I told the clerk that day, simply by scanning the shelves and flipping through books there as I learn from actually buying more conventional books at "normal" shops. Earlier in this book, particularly in the chapter about empathy, I quote heavily from the work of primatologist Frans de Waal. In The Peace Nook, I happened to encounter his newest book, *The Bonobo and the Atheist* (2013). In this book, de Waal argues that ethics and morals are not born out of religious doctrine, or any other man-made construct, but can be understood as a natural development of primate behavior, a development that has evolutionary, and biological, benefits. And it's maybe not just primates, either, as elephants are included in de Waal's book as examples of animals exhibiting empathy. We tend to believe, as humans, that our sense of morality, the sense that we must care for and do good to others, is a specifically human trait, one cultivated through time and effort. But de Waal provides ample evidence that many primates, primarily the bonobo, but also the chimpanzee and the gorilla, likewise practice and exhibit moral behavior. And they clearly don't have organized religion. Or a constitution, or carefully penned laws. Nor, for that matter, do they have a written literature, or even, it seems, complex language with which to tell stories to each other. But they know to help each other, to care for the weak, to have sympathy for those in need, and to punish those who harm the group. de Waal concludes not by arguing that human religion is useless and should be eliminated (on the contrary, he sees it as a key component in complex human society and hence relevant whether or not its dogma is *true*); however, he does argue that religion is not the reason why we humans act in moral ways as often as we do. The reasons are found far deeper, and reach back into our history (and genes) far farther than formalized religion does.

The first thing I thought when I read the back flap of de Waal's book, was "well, if he's right my entire argument is untrue." And, of course, I had to buy the book. Even though I don't write about religion (I write about literary fiction, about stories), part of my argument is, undoubtedly, that stories change the people who read them—change them for the better. But if de Waal is right, maybe that's not true at all. Maybe stories are simply entertainment, nothing more, and nothing less. Perhaps they don't make us more moral. Anomalies exist, but morality is inherently inside all, or most, of us from the start.

Hence, this closing chapter came about. Its main idea is based on an after-thought I had in The Peace Nook when I had thought this book was nearly done. (Ironic, since the thought didn't bring me much peace at the time.) I decided that I had no choice but to dedicate some words to the idea of morality and/or ethics and literature. Reading fiction *might* make one more thoughtful, or empathetic, or understanding of others; but does it make a reader more moral? Up to this point I've danced close to this issue, near to this hot button word, but avoided it. In this chapter I tackle it head on. Can literature make you moral? In what follows I provide a brief definition of morality and/or ethics, provide a quick-and-dirty overview of some of the major thinking of the past about literature and morality, and then connect the concepts to my own arguments here about literature teaching in the US secondary school and the problem of morality.

What is Morality? Ethics?

Morality is generally seen as a body of beliefs, standards, or values that determine or delineate what is right and what is wrong in a certain group, culture, or setting. Ethics is often used as a synonym of morality, but can also be understood as a branch of philosophy that studies or explores issues of morality, or the more defined, practical behaviors that determine a moral system. In common usage, morality is often associated with goodness and sometimes with religious doctrine, or semi-religious doctrine, such as the Golden Rule (do unto others, as you would have them do unto you). In school settings, moral and ethical education is sometimes dubbed "character education," particularly in elementary and secondary schools where morality and ethics are seen as the domain of families, not teachers. I will talk more about the secondary school version of moral teaching later in this chapter.

Morality and literature, or how literature can or cannot affect morality and the ethical behavior of readers has been a topic of interest for literally thousands of years. Plato and Aristotle debated the value of poetry over two thousand years ago; in 1955 Theodor Adorno wrote it was barbaric to write poetry after the acts at Auschwitz; Bruno Bettleheim (1976) explored how Freud's theories can help adults understand how fairytales teach children, as they undoubtedly are meant to do; philosopher and literary scholar Martha Nussbaum (1990, 1995, 1999, 2001) has written prolifically about how the liberal arts and literary study can affect human life in more practical domains—her *Love's Knowledge* (1990) in particular explores literary fiction and its moral influence; John Gardner (2000) wrote a controversial book about the morality of fiction itself (and the sad lack of morality reflected in much contemporary fiction in his opinion) and how it might encourage readers to such ends themselves; and Wayne Booth's *The Company We Keep* (1988) explores how and when reading fiction might be considered an ethical *act*, defined in a number of ways, but focusing on what happens to readers when they read. Many other philosophers and literary critics have also written about intersections, or the lack thereof, between literature and morality, including Kenneth Burke (1972), Jacques Derrida (1992), and Richard Rorty (1984). While I am no expert in the study of philosophy and literature, the upshot of many of these works is similar; while the text itself may not be "moral" or "immoral" it can produce such effects on human readers, if said readers consume the text in ways and with the means that allow it. Often, such consumption requires that the reader approach the fiction as an opportunity for personal reflection and consideration of options—he or she comes to fiction as a way to explore various ways of handing life's exigencies, before making requisite real-world decisions. So the text itself may not contain morality per se, but it provides an opportunity for human readers to hone their own moral, or ethical, responses. I don't think Frans de Waal would disagree with this possibility, as this theory doesn't assert that readers would not be moral beings without something good to read; it simply says that such reading can make us more moral, more ethical, more thoughtful, if we approach the reading act with appropriate respect, care, and openness. It's not a cause–effect situation (reading a good book does not make a good person); fiction can be more like a catalyst or prompt, if approached with the right frame of mind, and the appropriate intellectual and emotional resources. Maybe the bonobo simply doesn't need as much help as we do. Maybe that's why they never learned to read.

Wayne Booth in his book *The Company We Keep: An Ethics of Fiction* (1988) argues for the idea of literature having an ethical function, but only in concert with the needs and perspectives of the reader coming to it; the reader keeps the "company" of a text, and uses/reacts to that company based on his or her needs at that present time. Just as we can be influenced by human company, we can be affected by textual companionship. Hence:

> The fact that no narrative will be good or bad for all readers in all circumstances need not hinder us in our effort to discover what is good or bad for us in our condition *here and now*. . . . . I must leave it to each reader to practice an ethics of reading that might determine just which of these standards should count most, and just which of the world's narratives should now be banned or embraced in the lifetime project of building the character of an ethical reader.
>
> *(p. 489)*

Of course, in addition to assuming that good books are written, such an argument leaves much in the hands of a supposedly skilled, and thoughtful reader, who knows how to think about texts critically and carefully, a reader who it is assumed will have experienced along the way some education in literature and literary reading. Is this yet another argument for the continued inclusion of literature in the secondary school? For how can a reader come to a book with such careful intellectual and emotional readiness if he or she has never practiced such reading and response in the company of teachers or peers? Has never engaged in a rigorous and multi-dimensional discussion about literature in a classroom, reading group or a book club? Has never experienced how a literary text can inspire questions and conversations, in addition to raw emotions and suspenseful engagement?

Such is the argument of Northrop Frye (1964) in *The Educated Imagination* who describes how the so-called "educated" reader can both react emotionally to texts and critically analyze them, can be emotionally close to a story and simultaneously distance him or herself from it as necessary, in order to both understand the text personally and viscerally and connect it to a wider context, world, and audience. The educated reader can identify with a text without mindlessly imitating it; can critically analyze a text, without it becoming only fodder for an essay exam. A similar, albeit more contemporary, argument is made by theorist Deanne Bogdan (1992), whom I discuss in my book *Young Adult Literature and Adolescent Identity Across Cultures and Classrooms*. While Bogdan:

> agrees that reader-response approaches are valuable and appropriate for holistic, student-centered literature curricula, she worries that such approaches also leave teachers vulnerable to the accusation that they are teaching values and morals, or otherwise indoctrinating students into a particular way of thinking or being. She cites the earlier work of Northrop Frye to argue that the literature teacher must encourage and allow personal response, but also must teach students to be critical readers who can step back and detach themselves from a narrative in order to understand and experience it fully.
>
> *(Alsup, 2010, p. 8)*

In this previous book I seem to argue that such balanced teaching may be a way for teachers to "get away" with teaching for morality while not appearing to do so; such alternating between aesthetic and efferent readings can make the reading experience seem both emotional and intellectual, even if the emotional, Bogdan's so-called "actualization," (Bogdan & Straw, 1993) is what we are really after. Here I take a slightly different slant, as I argue that both the emotional and the intellectual are necessary components in the reading act if we wish for ethical or moral results; the reader may need to identify, empathize, and think critically nearly simultaneously in order to sort through narrative options or vicarious realities and make good personal choices. Fiction doesn't *make* you moral; it provides the opportunity for morality—or moral behavior—to result. But the continued teaching of literature is a necessary component in this process. While such literary experiences might happen independently with some readers, some adolescents who have reading parents or caregivers, many children and adolescents will need structured opportunities, and enthusiastic, model readers, to embody the possibilities for them. Therefore, I include my last model of the reading process, this time depicting how literature might lead to moral attitudes and behavior, as prompted by classroom literary experiences.

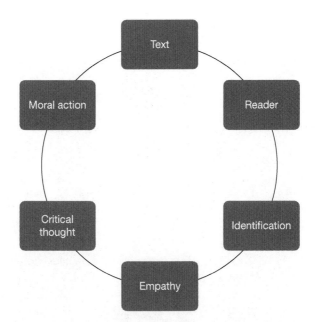

FIGURE 10.1 How reading can influence morality. In this figure, all aspects of the reading process, from identification through critical thinking, are enacted to result in some sort of ethical decision-making. There are no arrows used to indicate that the process is ongoing, reciprocal, and dependent on the surrounding context and reader dispositions. The process can also be halted at any point on the circle due to a number of factors, including lack of experience, interest, or opportunity.

The Problem with Morality in Secondary Schools

But there's a problem. Anyone who's ever walked into a middle or high school and been asked to teach kids about morality knows what I'm talking about. When the phrase "morality education" or "character education" is used in conjunction with public schools, the connotation is often religious education and the teaching (or indoctrination) of religious concepts or beliefs. This misunderstanding is just what de Waal was speaking of in *The Bonobo and the Atheist*: the knee-jerk assumption that all moral behavior and ethical decision-making is rooted in religious dogma. Or, in the case of public schools, the fear that it might be.

Ironically, schools have always trained students in so-called correct behavior, from following arbitrary rules such as walking in single file and not chewing gum, to sharing and not cheating on tests. At least the last two (sharing and not cheating) could be called moral, or ethical imperatives. Public schools seem comfortable being a training ground for controlled, proper citizens (see discussions of the hidden curriculum and moral education by Henry Giroux, 1983), but not claiming themselves to be centers for moral learning. The reasons are probably many, beginning with public schools being *public*, and not religious or private, and therefore vulnerable to criticism and even lawsuits if church and state lines are crisscrossed. A related concept more commonly discussed at the elementary and secondary levels may be "character education," a more abstract term that leaves out the word "moral" and hence smacks less of religion and didacticism and more of training good citizens. But these programs can be either thoughtful approaches to student personal growth, or just euphemistic covers for dogma or the teaching of thoughtless rule-following ensuring good student behavior as defined by the adults in charge, or even as a masked way to promote political conservatism. (To be fair, liberal education is often accused of doing the same, in reverse.) Perhaps the most famous of moral educators is Kohlberg (1958), who devised his stages of moral development to explain how morality might be understood as a psychosocial process occurring throughout the life cycle, without resorting to religion or subjective values to explain why some people are more moral than others. Kohlberg assumed that some of us just get stuck at those lower levels while others, more advanced, vault to the top.

However, morality and public education need not be enemies if ethics, morality and schooling are approached, as I do in this chapter, as an opening for student contemplation and educated response, not didactic, idiot-proof indoctrination. I, and many others, assert that a liberal education is a moral education, not in that it *teaches* what morality is and exactly what is right and wrong, but in that it strives to open the student mind to possibilities and potentialities and their consequences.

Literary study is one ideal way to open up such dialogue and intellectual exploration. Moral education doesn't have to be a discussion of whose values are right and whose are wrong; it could instead be immersion in the various possibilities and their pros and cons; narrative experience, while not completely a no-risk space, can open and sustain such opportunities. So in contrast to moral education leading to a restriction of beliefs and values, a liberal arts moral education opens up possibilities and introduces students to diversity and difference—in short, to the range of possibilities presented to them in today's word and what they might mean when translated into daily practice, behavior or decision-making. Nesteruk (2004) makes the argument that a moral education is not about teaching certain content but about "enabling dispositions" that "make possible a particular kind of practice, one that ask about the nature of the good life" (p. 69). To enable such dispositions students need to be exposed to new ideas, new narratives if you will, that confront or challenge their existing ones. While the possibility of narrative trauma exists (see Felman and Laub, 1992) whereby students are too shaken by a narrative to consider it intellectually, or, by contrast, decide to reject any literary experience altogether as too dangerous, risky, or painful, most literary fiction contains the potential for both emotional engagement and cognitive consideration.

Looking at morality education in this way might lead one to believe that the public school may be the best place for it, as it is filled with more diversity of belief, culture, race, ethnicity, gender identity and socio-economic status than perhaps any private or parochial school will ever be. In such a world of difference, could there be a better place to ask students to grapple with this difference and the solidity (or fragility as the case may be) of their own identities and identity positions? If we are not only to *teach* literature, but to teach students useful and appropriate dispositions to live in a diverse, complex, global, and increasingly uncivil and even frightening world, perhaps the time for a moral, liberal education has come. And fiction has a real place within it.

Why Worry About Fiction and Morality? Isn't Critical Thinking and Identifying with Characters Enough?

So after all this discussion, we may still be left to wonder, is reading literary fiction a moral act? Can it result in moral or ethical change? If so, can it likewise result in a decline of morality if the right literature is not read? Should this make teachers, parents and even adolescents themselves fear literature and narrative fiction?

I write this afterword in the days and weeks following the events in Ferguson, Missouri. An unarmed, young black man was shot multiple times by a white police officer, and unanswered questions and protests—some violent, some not—were ubiquitous in the weeks afterward as public perception grew that the officer at fault was not being held accountable by a racist, and militarized, police force. At the end of a faculty meeting one day, I spoke with a colleague about my project and how I was attempting to make a claim for the morality of literature, or at least, for the potential of a moral response to literature. My colleague answered by bringing up Ferguson. She said that one of the reasons Ferguson happened was because of the lack of opportunity to explore, intellectually and emotionally, various responses to challenges and even to trauma. Perhaps if such decision-making and response was practiced prior to real-life events occurring, fewer such tragedies would happen in the first place, or be escalated into further violence in their aftermath. Now this might be quite a stretch—of course, Ferguson, Missouri was caused by many other deep social problems and rifts that reading literature alone cannot begin to solve, not the least of which is institutionalized, entrenched and even normalized racism in the US. However, my friend and colleague had a point. Maybe if experiences of trying out potentialities, and thinking through narrative struggles, and experimenting through narrative experience, were more common-place, as opposed to a thoughtless consumption or imitation of texts and stories (or no reading at all), we humans would be better prepared to act in the face of real trauma and crisis.

In today's world there is much to be feared. Russia seems to be reclaiming its identity as a cold war enemy and the Islamic State is expanding its geographical and ideological control, while engaging in extreme, ruthless, and seemingly random violence. Terror alert levels designated by colors on charts that look like the old food pyramids confront us at the airport before we hop on a plane to go to a conference or on vacation. "Active shooter" drills are now as common in schools as tornado and fire alarms. Nowhere seems completely safe, and no one is safe from blame or consequence. How could reading a book really matter here? In February 2014, Stanford University's Center for Ethics in Society held a conference exploring the question, "does reading literature make you more moral?" Their answer, says reporter Paula Moya who reported on the event, "was a definitive no" (2014, p. 1). Not because literature doesn't matter, but because it doesn't provide *the* answer for a moral life, but instead provides a range of answers through which to sort. As Moya goes on to write, "because works of literary fiction engage our emotions and challenge our perceptions, they both reflect on and help shape what we consider to *be* moral in the first place" (p. 3).

Researchers Satterfield et al. (2000) attempted to discover whether people reading about challenging environmental issues (in their study, making sure salmon aren't blocked from their spawning grounds by hydroelectric plants) are better able to make more thoughtful and informed political choices if they read about the issues as narratives, as opposed to a series of facts. They found that, sure enough, the participants reading stories about the salmon were indeed more likely to be aware of the issue in the larger context of its importance; the *story* of the salmon seemed to help readers understand more deeply why it might be impor-tant that they are able to return each year. If such an experiment works with 239 readers at the University of Oregon reading—and thinking—about salmon, why can't we believe that young readers might also emerge deeper thinkers and feelers, more empathetic toward others, more ethical, and even moral people after engaging with narrative worlds in classrooms? I, for one, believe it.

References

Adorno, T. (1955/1983). Culture, critique and society. *Prisms: Studies in contemporary German social thought*. Cambridge, MA: MIT Press.

Alsup, J. (Ed.) (2010). *Young adult literature and adolescent identity across cultures and classrooms: Contexts for the literary lives of teens*. New York: Routledge.

Bettleheim, B. (1976/1991). *The uses of enchantment: The meaning and importance of fairy tales*. New York: Penguin.

Bogdan, D. (1992). *Re-educating the imagination: Toward a poetics, politics, and pedagogy of literary engagement*. Portsmouth, NH: Boynton Cook.

Bogdan, D. & Straw, S.B. (Eds) (1993). *Constructive reading: Teaching beyond communication*. Portsmouth, NH: Boynton Cook.

Booth, W.C. (1988). *The company we keep: An ethics of fiction*. Berkeley: University of California Press.

Burke, K. (1972). *Dramatism and development*. Worcester, MA: Clark University Press.

Derrida, J. (1992). *Acts of literature*. New York: Routledge.

de Waal, F. (2013). *The bonobo and the atheist: In search of humanism among the primates*. New York: W.W. Norton and Company.

Felman, S. & Laub, D. (1992). *Testimony: Crises of witnessing in literature, psychoanalysis and history*. New York: Routledge.

Frye, N. (1964). *The educated imagination*. Bloomington, Indiana University Press.

Gardner, J. (2000). *On moral fiction*. New York: Basic Books.

Giroux, H.A. (1983). *Hidden curriculum and moral education: Deception of discovery*. Richmond, CA: McCutchan Publishing Corp.

Kohlberg, L. (1958). *The development of modes of thinking and choices in years 10 to 16*. PhD Diss. University of Chicago.

Lewis, C.S. (1952/2002). On three ways of writing for children. In *Of other worlds: essays and stories*. New York: Mariner Books.

Moya, P.M.L. (2014). Does reading literature make you more moral? *Boston Review*. Retrieved September 1, 2014 from www.bostonreview.net/blog/paula-ml-moya-does-reading-literature-make-you-more-moral

Nesteruk, J. (2004). Liberal education as moral education. *National Civic Review*, 93(1), 68–72.

Nussbaum, M. (1990). *Love's knowledge: Essays on philosophy and literature*. New York: Oxford University Press.

Nussbaum, M. (1995). *Poetic justice: The literary imagination and public life*. Boston: Beacon Press.

Nussbaum, M. (1999). *Sex and social justice*. New York: Oxford University Press.

Nussbaum, M. (2001). *Upheavals of thought: The intelligence of emotions*. New York: Cambridge University Press.

Rorty, R. (1984). Deconstruction and circumvention. *Critical Inquiry*, 11, 1–23.

Satterfield, T., Slovik, S. & Gregory, R. (2000). Narrative valuation in a policy judgment context. *Ecological Economics*, 34, 315–331.

APPENDIX A

Sample Lessons and Activities for Teaching Literature to Encourage Identification, Empathy, Critical Thinking, and Social Action

A.1: IDENTIFICATION

Contributed by Chea Parton, Purdue University, formerly of Southern Wells Community Schools, Poneto, Indiana.

Steinbeck's *Cannery Row* and Characters Like Me

In an effort to help students understand that characterizing a person as a "good" or "bad" person based on their actions (like Mack and the boys stealing and manipulating people to survive in the novel) is not as simple as it seems, I asked them to pick a character they felt was most like themselves and illustrate the character from the book as well as their own personal character in symbolic terms to better understand why they identified with the character, how they are alike and different, and whether either of them should be characterized as a good or bad person. The actual assignment sheet is below.

Cannery Row final project

Throughout the course of our study of this novel, we've discovered that everything a person does says something about him/her. All of the characters in the novel are complicated; they have good qualities and bad qualities, much like all of us. For your final project, you will complete the following:

Character collage

- Make a collage of ten images (from magazines, drawn, printed) that symbolize traits of your character. You are not allowed to grab all ten from the Internet.
  - o These images will be largely based on the character's behavior and whether you feel they are "good" or "bad".
  - o Remember that a symbol is something that represents something greater and larger than itself, so these images need to have deeper meanings than "Doc collected marine life, so I included this picture of an octopus."
  - o Along with your collage submit a brief expository essay explaining the character of your chosen character and the choices of images that you chose to represent them.
- Make another collage of ten images (from magazines, drawn, printed) that symbolize traits of *your* character.
  - o These images should also largely be based on your own personal behavior. How does society view you? In what ways are you, like the character you chose, misunderstood?
  - o Remember that a symbol is something that represents something greater and larger than itself, so these images need to have deeper meanings than "I play basketball, so on my collage I included a basketball."
  - o Along with your collage, submit a brief expository essay explaining your own personal integrity and character as well as your choices of images to represent them.

My Character		Me	
Trait	*Symbol/Image*	*Trait*	*Symbol/Image*

A.2: EMPATHY

Contributed by Laura Whitcombe, McCutcheon High School, Lafayette, Indiana.

Zeitoun and Empathy: Sophomore English Class

Promoting emotional/social growth and empathy with literature: As students read they must keep asking themselves the question: What would I do? Why does Zeitoun make the choices he does? How do those choices affect his family? Students are asked to consider how they would react to a crisis like Hurricane Katrina.

Social action: Promotes awareness of the similarities between Islam and Christianity. Promotes awareness that Muslims have many of the same values that the rural public school students hold in their families. Promotes an understanding of how experiences can affect religious, and political beliefs.

Before reading: Students view an excerpt of the documentary *When the Levees Broke* from Spike Lee to set the scene of New Orleans leading up to and during Hurricane Katrina.

During reading: As we read the nonfiction *Zeitoun* by David Eggers, students are responsible for keeping up with study guide questions that focus on the events occurring with the family members within the novel.

After reading: Students will produce a time line using the TimeLiner program. This will connect the events of Hurricane Katrina to the actions of the characters in the book. For each date given in a chapter of the book students are required to provide an image, a caption, a web link, the page number, and the date of the event. This fulfills technological, research, and many other standards.

Focus and assessment: Essay quizzes will be used to focus on the big questions from the reading. The novel is organized into five parts. After each part students will write short timed essays. Essays will continue to develop the writing skills for persuasion. Students will organize their essays with a clear Claim, provide Data from the book, and interpret their data with a Warrant. Here are the writing prompts and question choices that students must consider, develop answers, and provide proof from the book to support.

- Part one: What kind of man is Zeitoun? What kind of friend would Zeitoun be? Would you want him to be your friend? Would you want to work for Zeitoun? Why or why not?

- Part two: How are the characters reacting to the crisis of the storm? Who is reacting negatively? Who is reacting in a positive way?
- Part three: How do the excerpts from the Qur'an comfort Zeitoun? How does Zeitoun's Muslim family react to events? How does Kathy's Christian family react? How do the Qur'an excerpts connect to events? What Bible stories compare to the excerpts included in the book from the Qur'an?
- Part four: Write a personal narrative or inner monologue from Zeitoun's point of view about all of the trials he and his family have been facing. Make sure to include examples from the text, especially from Part four, pages 203–290. Put page numbers in parenthesis.
- Part five: Write a letter in the voice of either Kathy or Zeitoun. If you chose Kathy, then write a letter to Zeitoun. If you choose Zeitoun, then write a letter to Kathy. Either apologize, forgive, or ask for forgiveness. Cover some of the following in that character's voice: How are they feeling? How is this affecting their friendship or relationship? Especially focus on part five pages 291–325.
- Post-reading: After reading the book students will read the news articles showing the domestic violence charges that Zeitoun faced after Hurricane Katrina. Answer the following prompts: Does this mean that Zeitoun is no longer heroic? Why or why not? What do you believe led Zeitoun to this behavior? Explain what incidents from the book may have influenced his state of mind? Do you believe that PTSD may have influenced his actions? How do you believe the events may have affected Zeitoun's religious beliefs? How do you believe the unfair treatment may affect his political beliefs?

Reference

Eggers, D. (2010). *Zeitoun*. New York: Vintage.

A.3: CRITICAL THINKING

Contributed by Shaylyn Marks, formerly of Westfield Middle School, Westfield, Indiana.

Group Project: *The Giver*

For your novel project on *The Giver*, you will be asked to think about various aspects of the novel in small groups with the hopes that you will be able to piece together the theme, and in turn, gain a greater overall understanding of the novel. To do this, each group will be responsible for a chunk of the remainder of the book. Each group will be asked to think about things such as vocabulary terms, plot, important quotes, theme, and develop discussion questions for the class. Not only will this be an assessment of your overall knowledge of the novel, but it will also be an assessment of your ability to work within a group and your ability to speak in front of a group.

The primary objective of this project is to develop a better overall understanding of the novel by analyzing some of the smaller parts of it. In addition, these presentations will serve as a great way for us to begin studying for our test on *The Giver*. Within each project, each group will be asked to think about the following:

- Vocabulary words
- Discussion questions
- Important quotes
- Plot
- Interactive activity
- Theme (last group)

In understanding that this project is not just about demonstrating your knowledge of the novel, but also your speaking skills, you will need to consider the following when putting together your group presentation.

- Eye contact (both when you are speaking and when other group members are speaking)
- Voice projection (make sure that everybody can hear you clearly)
- Getting the audience to participate in your presentation
- Keeping the audience's interest (the teacher is not your audience, the class is)
- Each group member needs to speak during the presentation
- Each group will be given no more than 20 minutes to do their presentation

Reference

Lowry, L. (1993). *The Giver*. New York: Houghton Mifflin.

A.4: SOCIAL ACTION

Contributed by Jeff Spanke, Purdue University, formerly North Montgomery High School, Crawfordsville, Indiana.

Community Discourse: Building Bridges with Literature

Course/instructional unit mission

This course seeks to investigate the various forms of injustice (social, political, interpersonal, etc.) to which world literature historically strives to respond. Through aligning students' reading, writing, and oral communication skills with the Common Core State Standards (CCSS), this course addresses community needs as a means to accentuate the themes of injustice pervasive throughout other literary (con)texts. By augmenting community engagement with classroom activities predicated on developing students' critical thinking and analytical skills, this course aims to cultivate not only better readers and writers, but more empathetic, compassionate, and empowered citizens.

Course/instructional unit themes

- What is my relationship to the world?
- What do I even mean by "world?"
- What do I like about my community?
- What do I not like?
- What aspects of my community can I influence?
- What aspects of my community can no one influence?
- Where do my beliefs come from?
- How have my beliefs changed over time?
- How do my beliefs match those of other people?
- How do my beliefs benefit others?
- How do they hurt others?
- How have authors I've read perceived their communities?
- What did they hope to accomplish by writing their stories?
- What injustices do I see in my community?

Building on students' interests/beliefs articulated in weeks 1–2, and based on their various community observations/perceptions of weeks 3–4, these weeks serve to identify various community needs and problems. Using literary texts covered in class as a springboard, students should spend these weeks locating, identifying, and describing various injustices manifesting in their community. Below is a sampling of the literature students might read and related issues they might choose to explore in their communities.

English 9/10: Mr. Jeff Spanke: Assorted course texts and uses

Literary text (fictional/ multimedia)	Social justice issues/themes discussed (abridged)*
SHORT STORIES	
"The Cask of Amontillado"	Envy, wealth, opulence, vengeance, ethics, mortality, plausible deniability
"The Most Dangerous Game"	Right to life, animal rights, gun ownership, power distribution, natural preservation, Darwinian economics
"The Gift of the Magi"	Poverty, beauty, unemployment, cultural standards of wealth, cultural traditions, materialism, gender equality
"The Sniper"	Military justifications, power distribution, familial relations
"Rights to the Streets of Memphis"	Poverty, racial relations, youth activism, non-violent protests, familial relationships
"The Euphio Question"	Drug use, capitalism, power relations, censorship, familial relations, role of education, health care
"2BRO2B"	Abortion, euthanasia, health care, plausible deniability, activism, mental health
"Harrison Bergeron"	Censorship, giftedness, poverty, science ethics, activism, mental health
"To Build a Fire"	"Local color," animal rights, wealth, knowledge vs. instinct, role of education, colonialism
"A&P"	Capitalism, minimum wage, consumerism, voyeurism, power structures, cultural standards of beauty
"Crossing the Border"	Racial relations, immigration, capitalism

"The Lottery"	Tradition, cultural preservation, activism, plausible deniability, loyalty, consumerism
"The Possibility of Evil"	Tradition, cultural preservation, activism, plausible deniability, loyalty, obedience, consumerism
"The Guest"	Immigration, role of education, war, activism, plausible deniability, racial relations, power distribution, obedience, loyalty
"The Hunger Artist"	Activism, cultural standards of beauty, exhibitionism, voyeurism, exploitation, animal rights, mental health, capitalism

POETRY

"Caedmon's Hymn"	Religious reverence, tradition, poverty, classism
"The Raven"	Isolation, cultural sources of fear, tradition, devotion to past, mental health
"Do Not Go Gently Into That Good Night"	Activism, personal responsibility
"An Athlete Dying Young"	Power distribution, cultural memory, classism
"Shake the Dust"	Activism, cultural standards of beauty, poverty, sexism, racism, classism, ageism, bigotry, homophobia, xenophobia, capitalism, mental health
Eddie Vedder: *assorted songs*	Activism, cultural standards of beauty, poverty, sexism, racism, classism, ageism, bigotry, homophobia, xenophobia, capitalism
"Like the Sun"	Personal responsibility
Emily Dickenson: *assorted works*	Activism, cultural standards of beauty, poverty, sexism, racism, classism, ageism, bigotry, homophobia, xenophobia, capitalism
"How to be Alone"	Activism, cultural standards of beauty, poverty, sexism, racism, classism, ageism, bigotry, homophobia, xenophobia, capitalism

LONGER FICTIONAL WORKS

Romeo and Juliet	Wealth, opulence, racial relations, violence, loyalty, fear of change, xenophobia, classism, sexism, ageism, sexuality, mental health
The First Part Last	Health care, racial relations, poverty, classism, role of education, familial status, sexuality
The House on Mango Street	Classism, racism, familial relations
Antigone	Envy, war, politic uncertainty, familial relationships, gender equality, mental health, tradition, pride, classism
Into the Wild	Activism, classism, mental health, capitalism, poverty, familial relations

FILMS/VIDEOS

The Truman Show	Capitalism, power differentials, gender equality, right to life, animal rights, voyeurism, exhibitionism, activism, consumerism
Crimson Tide	Loyalty, activism, war, political uncertainty, obedience
The Twilight Zone: assorted episodes	Cultural standards of beauty, capitalism, xenophobia, racism, sexism, sexuality, poverty
Friday Night Lights: assorted episodes	Racial relations, familial structures, obedience, loyalty, poverty, alcoholism, classism, sexism, sexuality, ableism, personal responsibility, capitalism, power structures, consumerism

* These issues/themes were assessed using a variety of formative/summative measures including essays, informal writing prompts, oral presentations, group discussions, action research, and formal examinations.

APPENDIX B

Additional, Related Sample Activities

- Anticipatory activities (respond to controversial statements; make personal connections)
- OQP (Observation, Question, Prediction) charts (focus on character feelings/actions)
- Group work and discussion
- Emotion pictures (respond to various pictures of faces; create own emotion pictures related to literature)
- Dialogue journals/dialectical journals
- Literary letters
- Perspective taking activities
- Think alouds
- Narrating images; telling stories about images/pictures
- Narrative retellings in students' own words
- Character identification/explication prompts
- Free writing/focused writing
- Imaginative responses (drawing, poetry, songs, role playing, reader's theater)
- Binary oppositions activity (complicate essentialist character labeling)

CONTRIBUTORS

Brittany Biesiada is a PhD candidate in English at Purdue University, specializing in 19th- and 20th-century American Literature. She received her Master's degree in English from Columbia University.

Paige Clinkenbeard is a graduate student at Purdue University, where she is earning her Master of Science degree in Curriculum and Instruction. She graduated from Purdue University with a Bachelor of Arts in English Education in 2010, and has been working as a high school English teacher ever since. Her academic interests include gender roles in YA literature, and specifically, how YA literature affects student perspectives of gender roles. She currently lives in Lafayette with her husband and son, Jackson.

Lydia Ann Drenth is an undergraduate student at Purdue University. She is studying Elementary Education. Prior to Purdue, Lydia lived in a small town in northwest Indiana called Lake Village and attended North Newton High School.

James Herman is a graduate student in Purdue University's Curriculum and Instruction Program, focusing on English Education. He received his Bachelor of Arts in Secondary English Education at Purdue. James has worked in higher education as a member of Purdue's Residential Life team for the past three years as a Resident Assistant and now serves as a Staff Resident for one of the residence halls on campus. Once he receives his Master's, he plans on either continuing to work in higher education or turning to educational research.

Natalie Lund is a third-year student in Purdue's MFA program and the fiction editor of *Sycamore Review*. Before attending Purdue, she taught middle and high school English at a charter school in Houston. She attended George Washington University for her undergraduate degree and is originally from Geneseo, Illinois.

Shaylyn Marks worked as a classroom teacher at Westfield Middle School outside of Indianapolis prior to pursuing a career in higher education. Shaylyn earned her undergraduate degree in English Education from Western Illinois University and her Master's degree in Language Education from Indiana University. In December of 2013, Shaylyn earned her doctorate degree in English Education, and is now pursuing publication of her research in multicultural literacy and education.

Taylor Norman is a doctoral candidate in English Education at Purdue University. Working primarily with narrative research, Taylor's research interests center largely around the collection and representation of stories told by teachers. Because of Taylor's experience as a rural high school English teacher as well as an undergraduate instructor in Purdue's teacher education program, explorations of teacher identity and its influence on teacher experience are her areas of scholarly interest.

Chea Parton is currently a graduate student at Purdue University where she teaches Literacy Theory for content area teachers. Before returning to Purdue, she worked in the secondary classroom, teaching AP literature, advanced composition, as well as sophomore and senior English. She is currently interested in exploring how the position of teacher, student, and adolescent are constructed by culture as well as how they affect each other in the classroom.

Tiffany Sedberry is currently a PhD student at Purdue University working on her dissertation. She worked as a classroom teacher at rural Indiana schools before returning to graduate school full-time. Tiffany earned her undergraduate degree at Ball State University and her Master's degree in English Education at Purdue University.

Kelly Shaw is a teaching assistant and graduate student working on her PhD at Purdue University. Prior to her work at Purdue, Kelly taught kindergarten for nine years in Indianapolis at Pike Township. She earned her undergraduate and Master's degree from Butler University.

Jeff Spanke is a doctoral candidate in English Education at Purdue University. His research interests include narrative ethnographical studies of alternative schooling, composition instruction, service learning, and pre-service teacher preparation. He is a former high school English teacher who currently teaches introductory composition courses at Purdue and serves as a research assistant for Purdue's Gifted Education Resource Institute.

Laura Whitcombe is an English teacher at McCutcheon High School in Lafayette, Indiana where she has worked for 21 years. She teaches speech, English 10, and senior British literature. Laura is also a member of the Indiana High School Forensic Association Hall of Fame as a 20-year Speech Team coach. She received her undergraduate degree in Secondary English, Theater and Speech Communication Education from Indiana University in Bloomington, Indiana. She earned her Master's of Science in Curriculum and Instruction at Purdue University.

INDEX

Made in the USA
San Bernardino, CA
26 May 2020